THE SHAMROCK AND THE SHIELD

Leo Reilly in his "Sunday best," circa 1894. It was the custom in those days to dress young boys in skirts.
Courtesy of Eleanore Hennessy..

The Shamrock
and the Shield

AN ORAL HISTORY OF THE IRISH IN MONTREAL

Patricia Burns

Véhicule Press

DOSSIER QUÉBEC SERIES

The publisher gratefully acknowledges the support of The Canada Council for the Arts for its publishing program, the Book Publishing Industry Development Program of the Department of Canadian Heritage, and the Société de développement des entreprises culturelles du Québec (SODEC). The support of the St. Patrick's society of Montreal has also made this book possible.

Cover art and design: J.W. Stewart
Cover imaging: André Jacob
Typesetting: Simon Garamond
Printing: AGMV/Marquis Imprimeur Inc.

LIBRARY AND ARCHIVES CANADA CATALOGUING IN PUBLICATION

Burns, Patricia
The shamrock and the shield : an oral history of the Irish in Montreal

(Dossier Québec series)

1. Irish–Quebec (Province)–Montréal–History.
2. Montréal (Quebec)–History. I. Title. II. Series

FC2947.9I6B87   971.4'280049162   C98-900227-6
F1054.5M19I62 1998

Véhicule Press
P.O.B. 125, Place du Parc Station, Montréal, Québec, Canada H2X 4A3
www.vehiculepress.com

Distributed in Canada by LitDistCo, and in the United States by Independent Publishers Group (IPG).

Printed in Canada.

To the memory of my parents,
Kathleen Murphy and
James L. Burns

Contents

Acknowledgements

I would like to most sincerely thank the St. Patrick's Society of Montreal and especially the Cultural Committee which gave me both financial and emotional support unstintingly. I am most grateful too, for the support of the following people: Kevin O'Donnell, former historian of the St. Patrick's Society, who worked so hard with me on this project and who did the interviews with Father Thomas McEntee, Jake McConomy, and Frank Hanley; Don Pidgeon, historian of the United Irish Societies, who was always available with his extraordinary knowledge of local history to answer my many questions; Father Thomas McEntee who knows absolutely everyone and can open doors that are not only locked but also portcullissed—he provided names and gave me help and encouragement; Sheila McGovern of the *Gazette* and Dr. Carl Christie who helped me gather information on the Liberator plane which crashed in Griffintown on April 25, 1944; my very tolerant daughter, Erin Olizar Fowler; other family members and friends who were so supportive and patient throughout; and the many people who allowed me to interview them and who permitted me to borrow precious family photographs—I will never forget their generosity. A final word of thanks must go to Simon Dardick, Nancy Marrelli, the excellent team at Véhicule Press and my readers who have made this third revised printing possible. I owe all of you a huge debt of gratitude.

Preface

When I was a young girl growing up on Mariette Avenue in Notre Dame de Grâce, my mother's admonition to my sisters and brothers and me as we headed off to school at St. Ignatius was, "Be careful crossing Sherbrooke Street." Years later and again living on Mariette I heard myself telling my daughter Erin, "Be careful crossing Sherbrooke." Some things had changed, however. My daughter only spent one year, grade six, at St. Ignatius. The reality of present-day Montreal dictated that she do her early elementary education in French. Another change was that, instead of attending the local high school, she went to a private school where I was confident she would receive what I considered a good old-fashioned type of education such as the nuns had dispensed in the fifties.

While interviewing Charles Blickstead, one thing which he said struck a familiar chord with me. His mother's parting, Irish-accented words to him when he left his home on Duke Street in Griffintown were, "Mind the harses," because in the early part of this century horses filled the streets of Montreal and runaway horses were a common threat.

My interest in oral history began rather subconsciously. I was lucky enough to have grandparents with whom I spent a lot of time. I used to listen to my grandmother, Elizabeth Normor Murphy from Belle Island, Newfoundland, tell about her days working as a governess for the Monsarrat family of Montreal. Lt.-Col. Charles Monsarrat was a civil engineer whose many projects included the Jacques Cartier Bridge in Montreal and the Quebec Bridge at Quebec City. As a much respected employee, my grandmother travelled extensively with the family. On a trip to Europe, she told me how thrilled she was to have seen the Prince of Wales and I still have a Limoges plate which she bought in France. My grandfather, Edward Murphy, was a Newfoundlander who came to Montreal in his twenties. He had fascinating stories about his days as a sealer, fisherman and miner. He told of men freezing to death on sealing ships. He told of his rum-runner brother who was shot and killed by the police and another brother who was lost at sea. He had stories of going to dances with his pockets full of screws and bolts which made a nice jingling noise and would ensure that the girls thought he was quite an affluent fellow. I heard about the parish priest who patrolled the roads with a big stick looking for couples enjoying pleasures denied to him. All these stories were told in the lovely accent of Job's Cove and invariably began with, "Me and the b'ys ..." His sister, Mary, had been plucked from the family by a recruiting team of American nuns and was whisked away to a convent in the States where she was trained as a nurse. She eventually left the convent and served as a nurse with the American Army in World War I. A tall, imposing, elegant lady, her voice, as I recall, had nary a trace of Job's Cove and on family visits to Montreal from her home in Cambridge, Massachusetts, she used to tell of her nursing experiences in the "war to end all wars." She spoke of soldiers being buried in France and the next day the rain would have washed away most of the soil covering their coffins; of having to treat the enemy soldiers only after the allies had been treated and of her mixed emotions when a wounded German officer who looked just like her father had to be put aside to be taken care of later. I wish I could relive those days and hear those stories again.

My father, a native Montrealer, strongly encouraged our Irish heritage. We were taken down to Griffintown to see plays and be introduced to the friends of my father's youth. Sitting in St. Ann's Hall, listening to song after song, I remember being gloriously happy that I was "Irish" and tremendously proud of being, "Jimmy Burns's daughter." I always felt that I was Irish and defined myself as such. It came as quite a shock to me when Mr. Shaw, the principal of St. Ignatius, came into Miss Walsh's grade seven class and asked all those who were Irish to stand up. I proudly rose from my seat. "Where were you born?" "Montreal," I replied, not knowing where all this was heading. "Then you're not Irish. Sit down." Meanwhile, there were concerts every year in honour of St. Patrick's Day. In preparation for this, the music teacher taught us innumerable Irish songs and we even learned the Irish national anthem, which I still remember.

I was also lucky enough to be taken by my Aunt Eileen to have lunch one day with Alan Murray at his house on Gladstone Avenue in Westmount. He had been one of two female impersonators in the Dumbells, a group which entertained the troops in World War I. It was an interesting lunch, with Mr. Murray giving his decidedly strong opinions on many subjects and people. Every time I pass what remains of Gladstone Avenue, I think of him and wonder what he is wearing up in heaven.

It is my belief that oral history makes our past come alive in a very special way by putting a human face on bare facts. The idea for this book was conceived by the Cultural Committee of the St. Patrick's Society and the interviews were begun in the summer of 1991. An attempt was made to find representatives from as many different groups as possible. I was always especially thrilled to find older people who could remember the Montreal of the early part of this century. Most of the people interviewed were of Irish origin but the few who were not had such strong attachments to or involvement with Irish neighbourhoods or organizations that their contributions were most welcome and appreciated. The ones who kindly agreed to be interviewed were amazingly forthcoming and it was a wonderful time in my life to visit these people in their homes and listen to their stories. I feel and hope that I made many new friends. I know that I learned a lot.

The approximately one-hour interviews were taped and later transcribed and edited. The edited version was then checked and approved by each person interviewed. I attempted, as much as possible, to check historical references and spellings of family names, and I apologize for any errors I may have missed. Editing was an especially difficult aspect of this project. The edited version had to retain the casual quality of spoken language and the individual speech patterns of the speakers while remaining easy and pleasant to read. I used my own judgement in deciding what to retain and what to change. I hope that the individuality of each speaker comes through and I accept total responsibility if I have failed in this regard. Although it is an accepted fact that the human memory is subject to errors, fabrications and distortions, I was surprised at the accuracy and honesty of the recollections of the people I interviewed.

Sadly, many of the people interviewed, including my own dear father, have since past away. May they rest in peace.

I hope you enjoy this book which for me was totally a labour of love and the realization of a life's dream.

Patricia Burns
Montreal, February 2005

Historical Background

There are many who believe that Irish immigration to Canada came in a wave in the 1847 period of exodus from the famine. There were many waves and different eras that brought the Irish to these shores. St. Brendan came in the first wave in 545 A.D. but settlement was not to be. Over a millennium passed before the Irish returned to Canada (Quebec) to settle with the French. This was noted by Advocate John O'Farrell in his address to the St. Patrick's Society of Montreal on January 15, 1872. O'Farrell noted that by the end of the 1600s approximately one hundred families, natives of Ireland, were among the French population of Lower Canada. With the British conquest of French Canada there were Irish soldiers who were part of the conquering army, as well as entrepreneurial Irish who followed and were noted in Montreal in 1761.

In Montreal, the first awareness of Irish Catholics in this city was in 1817 when Abbé John Richard Jackson, a Sulpician priest, became involved with them. Succeeding waves of Irish came to Montreal and by 1824 the Honourable Michael O'Sullivan, solicitor general and chief justice of Lower Canada organized the first St. Patrick's Parade in Montreal. In 1834 there was a sufficient population of Irish in Montreal to organize the St. Patrick's Society. St. Patrick's Basilica, opened on March 17, 1847, was the first church built for the Irish Catholics of this city. With the opening of the port of Montreal that spring came the Irish of the exodus from famine Ireland and with them the tragic epidemic that took approximately six thousand souls to a final resting place on Bridge Street in the area of the Black Stone.

The tragedy on Bridge Street was also the phoenix and coming of age for the Irish of Montreal. Within a generation the citizens of Irish heritage were active in all phases of Montreal's life. Griffintown became the place synonymous with the Irish and their vibrant spirit. Through their churches and organizations the Irish excelled in sports, debating clubs, musical and stage entertainment, judicial practice, medicine, entrepreneurial activities and politics. The people leading the Irish were, to name a few; Dr. Daniel Tracey, the first Irish-born physician to practice in Montreal who also founded a weekly newspaper called *The Vindicator*;

Dr. William Hingston, a president of the Dominion Medical Association and governor of the College of Physicians and Surgeons of Lower Canada; his son, Dr. Donald Hingston who was instrumental in the founding and development of St. Mary's Hospital, also a mayor of Montreal; Marcus Doherty, Queen's Counsel and appointed a judge of the Superior Court of Montreal; his son, Charles Doherty, a professor of Civil Law at McGill and later appointed the minister of justice for the federal government in 1911; James O'Donnell, the architect of Notre Dame Basilica in Old Montreal; Father Patrick Dowd, beloved pastor of St. Patrick's, inspiration and builder for his people; Francis Cassidy, head of the Bar of Montreal and also a mayor of the city; Charles Curran, one of the founders of St. Patrick's Orphanage; John Joseph Curran and his son Frank, both judges of the Superior Court of Montreal; and the great orator, parliamentarian and Father of Confederation, Thomas D'Arcy McGee. Great people are supported by many and the Irish populace worked to maintain a growing positive image.

The history of the Irish in Montreal involves some colourful characters; Charles "Joe Beef" McKiernan; Mary Gallagher, the Headless Woman of Griffintown; loveable characters of this generation like Father Francis Kearney of St. Ann's; flamboyant ones like Frank "Banjo" Hanley; sincere, dedicated ones like Thomas P. Healy; those who kept our history alive such as John Loye and Tim Slattery. To list all of them would fill this book but their names are noted in honours given to Grand Marshalls, Chief Reviewing Officers, Irishmen of the Year, presidents and officers of Irish organizations and other notations.

To remember our history demonstrates pride in our roots. Montreal's history has been embellished with many people from many lands, but only the Irish can bring them out onto the streets of Montreal in any weather on a Sunday closest to St. Patrick's Day.

Explorers we are born, on a quest through time, to show that humanity can be proud of our Irish roots.

Don Pidgeon
Historian, United Irish Societies
February, 1998

Leo Reilly

When Leo Reilly was born, Sir John A. MacDonald was prime minister of Canada. He remembered many important events of the early part of this century; World War l, the influenza epidemic of 1918, the Depression, and the vibrancy of the Irish Catholic community which was expanding at a great rate. For forty years he worked for the Federation of Catholic Charities and witnessed much pain and hardship during the Depression years. When his wife passed away, he lived for many years with his family until arthritis confined him to a wheelchair. He lived first at the Salvation Army's Eventide Home and when it closed he moved to the Father Dowd Home. This remarkable gentlemen lived to celebrate his 106th birthday on March 4, 1997 but passed away peacefully on May 25, 1997.

I was born on March 4, 1891 in the town of St. Henry which was not part of Montreal at that time. We used to have band concerts twice a week in the park on St. Antoine Street just west of where the Imperial Tobacco is now at Laporte Street and Agnes. When I was about five we moved up north to Laval Avenue near Rachel. Up there we belonged to a new parish by the name of St. Agnes on St. Denis Street. That church is today the shrine of St. Jude and is run by the Dominican Fathers.

My father came from Kilkenny, Ireland and my mother was a Farrell from Kingston, Ontario. Her family had come from Ireland to Newfoundland and then moved to Kingston. I've often wondered how it is that people come all the way across the ocean to meet someone here and get married. My father said that the voyage to Canada was rough and it took, I think, six weeks. I can only guess that he probably came here around 1887. My father worked for John Murphy's which, at that time, was on St. James Street near McGill. It later moved up to St. Catherine Street and Metcalfe where Simpson's was later located. Murphy's was a department store and my father was a salesman there in gents' furnishings.

There were five of us, all boys. I was the second child. I remember my mother saying once, "I wish I had a girl." My mother took sick and died about three or four weeks after I got married so she never knew any grandchildren. Our first house that I remember was on St. James Street near the Glen, opposite where St. Elizabeth Church is today. We had oil lamps and I remember doing my homework for school by the oil lamp. We had the old Quebec heater in the hall with the pipes running through the house.

We lived in the north end for a while and then we moved to St. Martin Street in St. Anthony's Parish. I was taken on as head altar boy and served with Father

Shea. Every June the altar boys were taken on a picnic and we used to go by streetcar to the Shamrock Lacrosse Grounds. The Jean Talon Market stands where the Lacrosse Grounds used to be. We had the Shamrocks, the Nationals and the MAAA (Montreal Amateur Athletic Association). Most of the sporting events like foot races and marathons were held at the MAAA grounds in Westmount. The Shamrocks were the best. It's funny but the Nationals had their grounds turned into a market too. One thing that happened at the National Grounds was that a Mr. Kennedy, a sportsman here in Montreal got the idea of running a Spanish bullfight because there was great interest in that sport at that time. Well, it was held on a Sunday, the place was packed and they had toreadors with Spanish costumes and everything. The band played, they opened the gate, and out walked the bull. It wasn't the bull that got mad; it was the toreador. The bull looked around, looked at the toreador, and munched on the grass. Then he'd move to another part of the field and keep munching on the grass. The crowd was in stitches laughing. They gave up and they found out the next day that the old bull had come from the abbatoir on Delormier.

I remember when I made my First Communion in St. Anthony's. A couple of days before, my mother got word that she had to leave and go up to Kingston for her father's funeral. The couple upstairs, Protestants by the name of Ward, told my mother not to worry. The night before my First Communion they took me upstairs and in the morning, they got me dressed and, of course, in those days you had a special uniform with a badge and everything. They took me to church for my First Communion and then in the afternoon they took me back for my Confirmation with Archbishop Bruschési. Then it was back to their house and they threw a party for me and my friends. Now that was given by a Protestant and I have never forgotten it. I went to school until about the sixth grade. Then, like many others, I went to work. In those days you had to pay for everything. There was nothing free.

St. Thomas Aquinas Parish was established in 1908 and disbanded as a parish eighty years later. I was away on a trip to Newfoundland and when I got back, my mother said, "Oh, Leo. We've got our own parish." I said, "Big deal." Anyway, I kept going to St. Anthony's. When St. Thomas Aquinas was having its first bazaar in the town hall of St. Henry my mother said, "Leo, you have to go to represent the family because the others won't go." I said that I would go. I went the first night. The second night, I was getting all dressed up and when my mother asked me where I was going I told her that I was going back to the bazaar. I went the third night and the fourth night too. She discovered that the reason I was getting dressed up every night to go to the bazaar wasn't the bazaar but a girl who lived next door to us. I went every night to the bazaar and I used to bring her home.

When I took this girl out on a date we'd go uptown. The streetcar would cost five cents each. We'd go to the corner of Bleury and St. Catherine and go to the Nickel Theatre. That's what you paid, a nickel to see a silent movie. So I had spent twenty cents so far. After we left the theatre, we'd go into an ice-cream parlour and have a banana split. Fifteen cents. You know what they are worth today? Four bucks! Then I'd buy a bag of candy for a dime. I spent sixty cents. The last of the big spenders. I remember one of the girls saying to me one time, "Gee, Leo, you spend an awful lot of money."

I got my spending money in those days by running messages for the ladies in the neighbourhood after school. We had the streets divided up: so many streets belonged to me, so many to somebody else. I'd call at each house and Mrs. So-and-so would give me a list of what she wanted at the grocer's, the butcher's and so on. When I got back she would give me a nickel or even a dime. Boy! Father Shea would hand me and the other two boys a dollar bill each on Saturday morning. Oh, we were rich, we felt like millionaires! We'd save our money and spend it on St. Patrick's Day. We used to get a holiday from school and go down and meet the parade. After the parade a bunch of us would walk all the way to Sohmer Park in the east end near Pie IX and Notre Dame. In those days that's where they had wrestling and all kinds of events before the Forum was built. We'd drop into a little restaurant and get some beans or something for lunch. Then we'd go to see the Young Irishmen Show in the park. When that was over at about five o'clock, back we went along Craig Street to another restaurant for something to eat and then we'd go up to the Monument National for the St. Ann's Young Men's Play. Percy Hyland used to be the producer. I think every parish in Montreal had an Irish show but we always made for the St. Ann's Show because they had all the big names. They were all real Irish shows showing what happened a hundred years before in Ireland. They always had the English soldiers and the hero who usually ended up on the scaffold and then everybody would sing, "God Save Ireland."

I decided to get really involved with the new parish of St. Thomas Aquinas and I can remember setting up chairs in the unfinished church and Father Tom in there too on his hands and knees washing the floor. Father Tom made me head usher in 1909 and I did that until 1920. I was over at that church every Sunday morning for seven o'clock Mass and I stayed for all the other Masses. I also belonged to the Aquinas Players. We used to put on plays and once I played "Charlie's Aunt." I wore my mother's clothes and I shocked her the night of the play. I had gone to see Jack Benny and I tried to copy him. During one scene I lifted up my skirts and among all the hanging lace I reached to get a flask and steal a drink. My mother was sitting beside Father Tom and thought I shouldn't have done that. Father Tom thought it was hilarious and told my mother that it was just a play.

In the First World War, we had conscription. I went up for an examination by six army doctors. Three of them told me, as I stood in a big room in my birthday suit, that they wouldn't give permission for me to join the army because I had a leaking valve in my heart and they thought that the sound of the big guns would kill me. The other three doctors thought I was healthy enough to go. I remember the head doctor, an Irishman, coming into the room and he lifted the roof with his language. He said, "If six doctors can't agree, send him home." One of the doctors said to me, "Go to your own doctor and have an examination and tell him you were refused on account of a leak in your heart." I was scared stiff. I went to my doctor. He examined me and said, "On the way home see if you can buy a horseshoe and put it over your bed. There's nothing the matter with you." So I've had a leaking valve in my heart since 1914. It was a good leak. One of the other boys who came with me was taken into the army but he never saw Europe. He did his training and became a messenger in one of the camps. I had a brother who went overseas and he got killed three days before the end of the war—on November 8, 1918 and the armistice was on the 11th. He was with the American Army because he had left Canada and was living in Kansas.

Right after the war we were hit with the black flu epidemic of 1918 which was worldwide. There was no going to funeral parlours. You died in the morning and you were buried at night. There was tragedy. There was one couple who were married in the church at eight in the morning and that same night the wife was a widow. The husband took sick at the reception and they took him out. They ran short of coffins. They were carrying the bodies up in every vehicle they could use. They would just put boards together. That was a terrible time. I know I postponed a trip to Louisville, Kentucky in June of that year. I waited until it was over because I was afraid that if I got sick in Kentucky I would be buried there. There was no fooling around.

I married a Miss Marie Archambault from just the other side of Kingston and we had three children. A French name but she was as French as I am. (laughs)

St. Patrick's Day

WEDNESDAY, MARCH 17th, 1915

THE DRAMATIC  SECTION OF

St. Ann's Young Men's Society

WILL PRESENT

"SPRIGS O' THE OULD SOD"

✦ A Charming Irish Drama ✦
Specially Written for the Society

By our late fellow-member, Mr. Jas. J. Martin

MONUMENT NATIONAL

ST. LAWRENCE STREET

Matinee at 2.15   Evening at 8.15

★★★

Plan of Theatre on view and Tickets for Sale at ALD. T. O'CONNELL'S ONLY, corner Murray and Ottawa Sts. from 7 to 9 P. M. Daily. (Phone Main 3833) after March 4th.

Matinee, 15c and 25c. Evening, 25c, 50c and 75c Boxes, $4 and $5.

★★★

❖GOD SAVE IRELAND.❖

MAURICE G. PENNELL,

Sec'y.

Cover of the program for the St. Patrick's Day performance at the Monument National, 1915. These shows usually involved a bad guy (English) and the good guys (Irish).
Courtesy of Thomas O'Connell.

The only one in her family who could talk French was her father, old Jimmy.

I was working in Redpath Sugar. I had been there for twenty-two years and they let me go. One man was fifty years old and he was just swept out. Another was forty-two years old. My own boss was forty and he was let go too with nothing. Those men could not get another job at that age. Father Tom (Heffernan) gave me a letter of recommendation for the Federation of Catholic Charities. Today I'm the sole survivor of the original group of FCC. It was formed during the Depression. Monsignor McShane, Father Tom Heffernan and Father John O'Rourke were getting desperate because all the parishes were ringing and asking what to do. They needed help and finally Ottawa sent down Charlotte Whitton and she told us that we had to form our own federation of charities. At that time there was the Red Feather but that was a Protestant group and their duty was to their own people. The Federation of Catholic Charities was then formed with a Colonel Ryan who was the president of a stock brokerage firm. All the parishes were asked to run a campaign. They hoped to get $75,000 and they got $115,000. They were on their way! That was around 1930. First they had an office on Drummond Street and later they moved over to Guy Street. They made me a welfare worker looking after St. Mary's Parish in the east end. Some of the other parishes in my area were St. Aloysius, St. Brendan's and St. Dominic's on Delormier.

People would come down to the office and register and tell us what they needed. We used to give them orders to buy at a grocery store within their parish which was good for everything except beer. At that time we moved our office to Cathcart Street and then to Philip's Square and finally back to St. Marc Street. The staff got to be quite numerous. At the beginning people used to call in and want to give us clothing and we had to pay a carter to pick it up and then have seamstresses and cobblers to repair everything. Some of the clothing that was sent in was a disgrace. Why they expected poor people to wear those clothes…Finally we stopped that and made an arrangement with Eaton's. The people would go down to Eaton's and pick out a new coat or whatever they needed in clothing and we would pay for it. One time Mrs. McLaughlin who was in charge at that time told us to go easy because it was the end of the month and there wasn't much money left. When I went in on Monday I was called in and she said, "Mr. Reilly, you were at the meeting and I asked you to be very careful with the budget. You have given out twelve orders for winter overcoats just this morning. I think you want to ruin us. Why did you do it?" I said, "They needed them, walking all the way down from St. Brendan's in little sweaters with nothing on their feet except an old pair of shoes in the snow." We gave them everything they needed. I worked there for forty years and I learned one thing about charity—there are three kinds of people. The first one is the real honest one and needs help. Then there's the second kind, the chiseler. If you don't watch them, they'll take your teeth. The third type is the one who is too proud to ask for charity. I had one case which I remember well in Outremont. I went in to work one morning and saw the name of a man needing help on my desk. I'd known the man for many years. He was originally from St. Thomas Aquinas and had moved to Outremont. When you went into his house you walked on beautiful rugs and the furniture was out of this world, the living room, the dining room, the bedrooms—everything was class. So I went to his house and when he opened the door he said, "Oh, Leo. It had to be you." I walked in and looked around and said, "Johnny, where is all your furniture?" He said, "Leo, I've been selling my furniture for three years. I got caught in the stock market crash and then the Depression. I lost my job and I sold everything. Now I've got nothing left to sell." All he had left was old furniture and oilcloth on the floors. I told him he was a damn fool and that he should have come to see me sooner. He would never get his good furniture back and he probably didn't get too much for it when he sold it. I put him on the list and we carried him for about a year. Finally we got him a job and, to his credit, every campaign after that he sent us a cheque for fifty dollars but he was just too proud to ask for help when he needed it.

I lived for thirty-five years in the same apartment on Côte St. Luc Road. After my wife died I told my daughter Estelle that I was going to take a bachelor apartment and she said, "You're not going to live alone. We have an extra room." So I went to live with her family and about two years after that they said, "Dad, you're going to get real fresh air. We're moving to Sutton." I said, "You're not taking me to Sutton. I'm a city slicker and I'm going to die a city slicker." I went to Sutton anyway and stayed for quite a while. Then I went to live with my other daughter who was a nurse at St. Mary's. When my arthritis got too bad I moved to the Eventide Home where I stayed for six years.

I've never been to Ireland. I spent ten winters in St. Petersburg, Florida, with some members of the St. Ignatius Senior Citizens' group. Now I wish that I had hit the other side instead of going there all the time. I could have seen Dublin and Kilkenny where my father was born. I also wanted to see London, Paris and Rome but I never crossed the ocean.

I don't know the secret of why I've lived to be over a hundred years old. I've had women both here at Father Dowd and at the Eventide Home where I used to live say to me, "Mr. Reilly, I don't want to live to be as old as you. It's too long to live." I said, "Why not if you're getting around? You're going to be a long time dead." There was another woman over at the Eventide, a real Irish woman, and she asked me which county of Ireland I had been born in. So I looked at her and I said, "Which county was I born in? Well, I'll tell you. I was born in County St-Henri de Montréal."

Leo Reilly celebrating Canada Day in 1993 at the Father Dowd Home. Born on March 4, 1891 when John A. MacDonald was Prime Minister, he was rejected for military service in World War I for health reasons, but lived to the fine old age of 106 with his "weak" heart.
Courtesy of Leo Reilly.

James Lawrence Burns

James (Jimmy) Burns was born in Point St. Charles in 1903. A few years later the family moved to Griffintown where he was enrolled in St. Ann's Boys' School. His academic career was cut short because, like many others, he was forced by family circumstances to go to work at the age of twelve. Later on, he took advantage of night school to complete his education. Eventually he began working for CPR at Windsor Station and he worked there until he retired at the age of sixty-five. Jimmy Burns was active in amateur baseball and hockey in his youth and maintained a lifelong interest in St. Ann's Parish and the St. Ann's Young Men's Society.

I was born on Ropery Street. From there we moved to Centre Street and then to St. Columban Street, all in Point St. Charles. I think it was in 1909 that we moved to Griffintown and I was entered in St. Ann's Boys' School in the first grade. This school was located on the corner of Young and Ottawa and was a three-storey building with a stone front. The first two levels were devoted to classrooms and the top level was a meeting hall where dramatic productions were put on and political meetings were held. The school was run by the Christian Brothers and many of them were either from Ireland or of Irish extraction. Were they strict? Well, they had to be. (laughs) In Griffintown they had to be strict but we had a variety of teachers. Many of them were very well educated and kind, and others were tough.

The school took an active interest in sports like hockey, lacrosse and baseball and, although the school yard was small we had a hockey rink in the winter and so a lot of boys from Griffintown became good hockey players. The whole area was heavily populated and was thick with talent in sports and other things.

One of the houses we lived in had no electricity and light was provided by coal oil lamps. When you went into a room, you had to strike a match to find the lamp to start with and then put the lamp on and tone it down so that the wick wouldn't smoke the chimney. Then you had to put it back on the shelf without dropping it or you wouldn't have any light at all. So these were the conditions we lived with before the days of modern conveniences. Saturday morning was the day my mother selected to do the family washing. Well, I was off school Saturday and my two sisters and I were detained in the house to help with the laundry. It was quite a setup. You had to get three chairs and place a wooden tub on the chairs and then heat water on the iron stove which you used for cooking, winter and summer. When this tub was set up and filled with water, you had to bolt a wringer on to it and then my mother would get a big washboard and a big bar of soap and proceed to scrub the clothes. When the clothes were washed they had to be put through this wringer manually, you see, before they were hung out to dry. So that was a long procedure and certainly in contrast with the way you do things now. I think, though, that these conditions prevailed in other parts of Montreal, too.

To give you an idea of what a dollar was worth; I went to work for the CPR as a junior clerk in 1916 and my pay was twenty dollars a month. We got paid in cash on the last day of the month. We signed the payroll and there were no deductions for unemployment insurance, income tax or anything like that. You got your twenty bucks and that was it. There was no such thing as a welfare program. The rent for a house wouldn't be very much but still, the poor labourers didn't get high wages either. Most of the property in Griffintown was owned by Irish landlords who generally lived in the neighbourhood.

When school finished for the summer, some of the people who were better off went to Chateauguay where they had summer homes but most of us hung around the streets every day and we'd make money however we could. We might pick up bottles and bring them up to the junk store and get some money. In the wintertime people could leave the milk between the doors but in the summertime they used ice boxes to keep the food cool. There were ice deliveries in the district but if someone ran short of ice, they would pay me a nickel or a dime to go and pick up some ice and I would deliver it to them in a little wagon. In those days, Donnelly's controlled the ice supply. They had a trucking business which was their main work but they also had a big ice house in their yard on Murray Street. Men would cut huge blocks of ice on the river and it was brought to Donnelly's and stored in sawdust until the summertime when it would be broken down into smaller blocks and sold to the public.

I don't remember celebrating Dominion Day but we used to celebrate Victoria Day in an unusual way. The drinking element set fire to all the junk shops around the district and you can be sure that the police were busy racing around. There were also many bonfires on Victoria Day but they were mainly of interest to the kids and people would go around collecting junk from people to burn.

I was in with a good crowd in Griffintown—the Brackens, the Taughers, the Consedines, the MacIntyres and fellows like that. We had our own baseball team which we called the Orioles. We played exhibition games in places like St. Henry. There was no shortage of fun either. If you got a gang in a doorway, there was always someone who could play the mouth organ and some of them were very good at it.

One thing about Griffintown was that we provided our own music. In the

"Good Old Griffintown," March 13, 1932.
James Burns dressed for the annual parade in Shamrock-bedecked
top hat, dark coat, white scarf and carnation.
The men of the St. Ann's Young Men's Society prided themselves
on their fine appearance and proper comportment in the parade.
Courtesy of the Burns family.

summertime with the windows open you could hear women singing all over the place. You'd be in the yard and hear "The Rose of Tralee" from "Mary Callaghan" and then "Mary Muldoon" would be singing "Danny Boy" so you didn't need a radio.

When someone died, the wake was usually held at home. There were funeral homes starting up but they weren't used as they are now. The body would be placed in the living room and crepe would be hung on the front door. They were handy to note because if you were up at a show uptown and weren't in any hurry to get home, you'd go into a wake and, if it were somebody who was well known, you'd meet all the famous sportsmen and get into a lot of good conversation in the kitchen. Sometimes the place would be packed and people would be everywhere—in the kitchen, the corridor, sitting on the steps. They were gathering places for conversation, you see. You might get talking with a bunch of fellows and they'd be talking about the lacrosse game last week that they lost or some prize fight. Of course, when they went in they expressed sympathy to the family but then the conversation drifted to whatever subject was brought up. The family would supply food, sandwiches and all that and alcohol if they had it. It was tiresome for the family because they'd be up all night and couldn't get much sleep. The coffin would be open and the wake went on for two days and then the body would be brought to church and to the cemetery.

Most people who died had some form of life insurance. If they didn't it was just their tough luck. There was a certain amount of benevolent activity. The Ancient Order of Hibernians would collect money to help their members and other groups gave similar help but there was no government assistance like we have now. St. Ann's Church would give all the help they could and a lot of people used to go there to borrow money but they were limited in what they could do.

When my father was working as a labourer in a steel mill on St. Patrick Street a heavy piece of metal fell and crushed the lower part of his leg. His leg was amputated below the knee and then gangrene set in and they had to amputate the entire leg. He was a big, strong, six-foot man and he survived that but he couldn't be fitted for an artificial leg and he lived with a lot of pain for the rest of his life. He was on crutches for about twenty-five years until he died at the age of seventy-five. Now, being on crutches made it difficult to get employment. The fact that you were a labourer was bad enough but if you were crippled.... He finally got work with the City of Montreal lighting the lamps at construction sites on city streets in the summer, and minding the furnaces at the revenue offices on Commissioners Street.

My father's accident dictated my whole existence. We first lived at two different locations on McCord Street near the church. Then we moved to Eleanor Street where we had a very nice house. From there we moved to Ottawa Street where we had a small house and it was there that the family broke up. My mother took my younger brother, Harold, and moved to St. Mary's Parish in the east end. My sister did the cooking for us until she got married. I then boarded with a family up the street, not far from where my father lived alone. I was in daily contact with him and I helped him as best I could but after I paid my board I didn't have much scope to spend money.

I had about six years of formal schooling and then I went to work. Brother James brought me up to the CPR when I was twelve years old and got me a job in the Accounting Department. Most families who could afford it sent their kids for an education but some of my friends went to work very young. One friend went to work for Dow Brewery and did very well but others had trouble getting work.

When the Redemptorist Fathers first came here from Belgium, some of them couldn't speak English but they were given the job of running St. Ann's Parish and they did a very good job. It was to Father Edward Strubbe's credit that so much was developed for the young men. He was the spark plug that got many things going. A school was built and then the four-storey Young Men's Society building. You had to join the St. Ann's Young Men's Society to participate in activities and it brought the kids together. You were given a job and taught how to speak in public. We didn't have professional coaching but you learned to speak by listening to better speakers who were brought in. We also had debates and we had to learn the rules of debating. There was no gambling or drinking allowed at the hall. Even on New Year's Day you got ginger ale and cigars and there was very close control. When you went somewhere else where there was a lot of booze, you had the training from St. Ann's to use your head. One very important feature was the Dramatic Society. They generally put on three productions in the parish during the year at the school hall but the St. Patrick's concert was the big event and was presented at the Monument National on St. Lawrence Boulevard. This concert drew people from all over the city. There are many people who still remember when whole families would go to see either the matinée or the evening performance. Schoolchildren were taught by the nuns and would sing and dance at this show. The kindergarten children were always a star attraction.

There was always a lot of traffic around the priests' house behind the church because the Redemptorists were missionary fathers and many of them came up from New Brunswick and other places and they would stop in Montreal for a few days before going on. The Redemptorists preached religion to you. When they got up to talk they could tell you white from black. (laughs) They used to quote the Scriptures, "If your right eye scandalizes you, pluck it out. Better to go to heaven with one eye than to hell with two." Things like that. They really laid it on but they always commanded respect. There were a lot of people in Griffintown who became alcoholics and who would never accept to be cured in spite of the fact that the Temperance League tried to get them to stop drinking for six months and then renew for a year and so on. These things helped but a lot of good people that I knew just drank themselves down the drain.

When I was going to school, we used to walk in the St. Patrick's Parade on the day itself. You left school and walked. Later on when I was working I was able to get permission to take the day off to walk. They stopped that after a while because if they gave the Irish a holiday on St. Patrick's Day they would also have to give a day off to the French to celebrate St. John Baptist Day. That (having the parade on the 17th) was changed by the historian John Loye when he wrote up the constitution for the United Irish Societies. When I was a young teenager the parade consisted of all the parishes in the city. Each parish had a band and a marching unit and they all converged on Dominion Square where they proceeded along Dorchester to around Atwater and then turned on to St. Catherine Street and walked to Philip's Square. A lot of people looked down their noses at the parade because there'd be a lot of people who would drink before they went in the parade but St. Ann's was always able to put in a good unit and keep the drunks out. We had young kids of eighteen or nineteen years of age and we had marshalls to control them. We had to wear a navy blue coat, top hat and a carnation. That was it. It made a good showing and we always had a good band like the fireman's band which was the best one in Montreal.

Many of the people of Griffintown earned their livelihood by working for the City. They'd own a horse or two and a wagon and would shovel snow in the winter and do construction work in the summer. The horses were kept in stables in the back yard. Tommy Maguire had about six horses and wagons. He also had horse-drawn cabs which serviced the Ritz Carlton Hotel. The Maguires and Billy Hushion were in that class and later Hushion went into partnership with another man and they formed Murray Hill Limousines. All these horses in

Griffintown needed a lot of care. They had to be taken out and washed and shoed. There were horse-shoers in different parts of Griffintown. Tommy Maguire would often ask me to bring one of his horses over two streets to where the shoemaker was. The horse was tame and only needed a halter so I'd steer him over to have him shoed and then he'd put me back up and I'd ride him back. On St. Patrick's Day, every kid's ambition was to ride a horse—to get out there decked in green and race around the place. I remember riding a horse across Dominion Square when I went to meet the unit in the parade. There was always a lot of excitement. Some people had nice horses, well groomed, but others didn't look too hot but the kids didn't mind as long as they could ride. You had to have a saddle and behave yourself. Mr. Cleary, who worked for the Montreal Light, Heat and Power, lent me a saddle one year from their stable on Ottawa Street and he told me to bring it back after the parade before the day staff came on so they wouldn't know it had been taken out. So after riding that bloody horse all afternoon, I was tired and went to bed early. I woke up, very wide awake and looked at the clock. The hands were straight down and I thought it was six o'clock in the morning. I got up, washed, and carried the saddle along Ottawa Street and a cop was looking at me as if to say, "Where the hell are you going with that saddle at this hour?" So, I got down to the stable and hammered on the gate to try and get in. The watchman was asleep and when I woke him up he said," What are you doing here?" I said, "Well, Mr. Cleary loaned me the saddle and I'm bringing it back." He said, "Why don't you bring it back in the morning?" You know, it wasn't six o'clock in the morning. It was half past twelve. So that was my fault. I should have looked more closely at the clock.

The cops patrolled all the time. They had to cover a certain territory after leaving the station. They would check the stores and factories and keep their eyes open for trouble. It was bitterly cold in winter down by the Lachine Canal and it was a lonesome district too. If it was a very cold night, sometimes the policemen wouldn't like to patrol but instead would visit the place where my father worked and sit and talk with him. They'd spend an hour or two and then go back to the station. When I went to help my father they'd be there talking to him with their overcoats on the table along with their guns.

Most of the policemen were Irish. That was the advantage of having Mr. O'Connell in authority because he got jobs for the Irish. Their work was tough because some of the men in Griffintown were tough guys, you see, and they wouldn't come down to the station willingly. The more cops it took to bring you to the station the greater your reputation as a tough guy. Those cops had to be able to take care of themselves. If a policeman was called to arrest his brother he'd probably send him home instead of bringing him to the station. There were many fights between the cops and people in the district. Some of the policemen were well liked and others weren't too popular because they were too tough.

Any organization that had to do with Irish independence usually visited Griffintown and spoke to people about helping out. There was one group which arranged a trip to Ogdensburg in 1919 to see Eamonn De Valera who was smuggled out of Liverpool on a boat and brought over to the States. He wasn't allowed to visit any colony of the British Empire so the dinner and talk were held in the States. I went with Eddie Collis. One of the main reasons we went was that we both had train passes. Otherwise, I don't think we could have afforded it. There must have been a couple of hundred in our group. De Valera spoke to us all and thanked us for our cooperation. Later, we had a chance to shake hands with him. I was only sixteen years old at the time but I remember that De Valera was a big, tall, scholarly looking man who was a good speaker. He thanked the people of Canada for what they had done. It was an interesting visit for me and I felt privileged to hear him talk. *

There was a certain amount of anti-British feeling in Griffintown because of the historical treatment that Ireland received from England. We heard stories from people who came from Ireland. Jack Carroll was born in Antrim and he used to tell us that when he was a kid the police would break down the door and rush in as the family was sleeping. They'd rouse them all up in their search for some guy they were after. Jack said that there was always a lot of interference from the police. When I went to work for the CPR I noticed that if the mainly English and Scottish people who were in power knew you were Irish Catholic you sometimes didn't get the best treatment. You certainly wouldn't get preferred treatment. It was different when Shaughnessy was in charge but that changed when he left. **

During the First World War, the Irish Canadian Rangers, an Irish regiment, was formed under the control of Irish-Canadian officers. The recruits were boys from different areas of Montreal. A full regiment was sent over and they were paraded through Dublin, perhaps in an attempt to suck in some of the Irish to join up. When the regiment got to England it was disbanded and the soldiers were sent to join other regiments. That did not go over too well here and some of the officers quit. It was a typical British way of doing things; I guess they couldn't trust this regiment.

I appreciate the training that I received through the St. Ann's Young Men's

Society. I was really living in two worlds. In Griffintown with its mainly Catholic population, we were protected to some extent, but when I started work at the age of twelve, I was living with an adult population because an office with eighty employees might have only two office boys. I listened to adult conversations all day and one of the things I got into was gambling. The adults in the office were subject to a great deal of supervision by the office manager. If you left your desk for half an hour they'd want to know where you had been. You were allowed fifteen minutes to go to the washroom and if you disappeared for longer than that there was trouble. They had no control over the office boys because we were going around the building all the time. So the staff would get information about a certain horse that would probably win a race. This information would be sent by wire from New York. While making my rounds, I would sneak across the street near Mother Martin's Restaurant to visit the bookie. There was a barber shop in the front and a pool room and a bookie in the back. In the bookie's office they had all the entries for all the American tracks around the place. Everything was posted—the name of the horse, his weight, track conditions, the jockeys. I'd study all this information and relay it back to the office staff and on their lunch break they'd go over and place their bets. A lot of people played the horses and there were bookies all over the place. We used to take a special train out to a racetrack in Dorval and we'd get tips from the waitresses down at the restaurant at Windsor Station because a lot of racetrack men would go there to eat. There were racetracks all over the city. Mayor Drapeau put an end to all that and it was a good thing because Montreal was becoming an open gambling spot. During World War II the military would complain because the troops would come in here with money and get fleeced playing barbotte.

Dancing was a popular pastime in Montreal in the twenties and thirties because there were dance halls all over the place like the Majestic Hall on Guy Street, Wood Hall in Verdun, Stanley Hall on Stanley Street and a big place down around Bleury Street. These places were in operation every night. Parishes would also rent these halls for dances when they wanted a big crowd. When you went to a parish dance you'd meet people from that parish but at the other dances you'd meet people from all over the city. There were a lot of contests and, one in particular that I remember was held at the Orpheum Theatre on a Sunday night. They were having a dance contest for the championship of the city and that place was jammed right up to the rafters. There were different styles of dancing; like fancy dancing and waltzing. The judge was Professor Frank Norman who was a dance teacher. We had two excellent dancers from Griffintown who used to compete, Billy Regan and Patsy Donahue.

Griffintown was, you might say, a depressed area and during the Depression it meant that you had less than you had before. It was sad to see many well-educated people who were broke and bumming the price on the street. In my case I was very fortunate. I always had a job from the time I started working at the CPR until I retired. I never had to go around looking for a job. A lot of the problems with young people today is that they can't get employment. Idle hands can get you in trouble.

* De Valera became president of Sein Fein in 1917. Sent to jail in 1918, he was eventually sprung from Lincoln Jail in 1919 by Michael Collins. He then left Ireland and visited the United States to mobilize American support for Ireland's claims. Irish Americans, always generous, came through and, in appreciation, on July 4th, 1921, the Stars and Stripes was flown from the Mansion House in Dublin on De Valera's orders.

** Thomas George Shaughnessy, an Irish American from Milwaukee, became president of the Canadian Pacific Railway when William Van Horne retired in 1899. His war efforts during World War I led to his being created Baron Shaughnessy of Montreal and Ashford, County Limerick (Ireland) in 1916.

The Hibernian Knights marching in the St. Patrick's Day Parade
in Montreal. They were the ceremonial branch of the
Ancient Order of Hibernians, a Roman Catholic fraternal
order which strongly supported Irish independence.
Courtesy of the Burns family.

Sarah Layden

Sarah Layden spent her youth in Northern Ireland and came to Canada in 1928. This was not a good time to immigrate as Canada was just about to enter the Depression years. She describes her life in Ireland at the beginning of the century and the difficulties she experienced along with so many others in the thirties.

I was born in County Antrim in September, 1906. Things were very bad over there. We used to have the British soldiers come in the middle of the night looking for guns and ammunition. They'd get us out of bed but there was just my father and five children. My mother died when we were very young. A couple of times they ransacked the house when I was alone. Quite a few of my friends were picked up by the soldiers and some got away to the States before it happened to them. Things were really bad. If you were a Catholic, you got nothing. We had Protestant neighbours and we got along very well. We had the odd fight. They would curse the Pope and we would curse King Billy and then we'd have a fight and then that was it.

When I was young we used to go to dances in Ireland. We weren't allowed out of the hall until six o'clock in the morning. They didn't want couples on the road at night so if you wanted to go early you had to leave before midnight. That was the rule put down by the priests. I've seen me coming home so tired and I had to work in the fields the next day. I could hardly see what I was doing. Our family didn't have a farm but we worked on farms. It was hard, hard work. There was no end to the day. When the weather was good they just took all they could out of you to get the day's work done. I milked cows and put them out in the field and brought them in again. Planting potatoes was very hard. You put them in a foot apart and if you were going down the hill you were bent right into the ground carrying the box of potatoes and putting them in. We'd go to bed at ten or eleven o'clock because it was clear and they'd keep you working in the fields as long as they could. There was no such thing as hours.

When we went to church, the women sat on one side and the men on the other. Even if you were married, you wouldn't sit with your husband. I couldn't get over it when I went home to Ireland for a visit. They were *still* doing it. The priest didn't like us mixing with Protestants and on St. Patrick's Day if you weren't covered with shamrocks the priest just bent down and pulled up a handful and put them on your coat. The priest had a lot of power but I think it was a good thing. Today there's no respect for anything. If you met a priest in Ireland you got down on your knees because he might be carrying the Host.

Even if it was pouring rain they all got down on their knees.

When I first came to Canada I worked in private homes as a maid. Cleaning has been my job most of my life. The first family wasn't good. They lived on Old Orchard in N.D.G. When they went to a movie I would stay home and mind the baby. After I put it to bed I would go to sleep and this woman would wake me up when she came home and make me run her bath, and then I had to wait until she was finished so I could clean the tub. The other families I worked for were very nice to me. It was really hard work though and altogether different from Ireland. There was a lot more work to be done here and the places were bigger. I was very lonesome at the beginning and I wanted to go back to Ireland but I never had the money. Even when my father died I couldn't afford to go back home and that was really depressing. The first winter here I thought I would freeze to death. So much snow and no way of cleaning it, not like today.

We used to go to dances at Seigneurs Hall and Majestic Hall and other places. At one of the dances there was a Miss Downey who was Irish. She had a stick and if couples were too close, she'd separate them. I met my husband at a dance at Seigneurs Hall and we got married in 1930. He was James Layden from County Derry. My son, the oldest, was born in 1933 and I also had five daughters.

I felt very lucky when I got a job in the Northern. My husband worked there too. They didn't let you work if you were married so they laid me off. Two weeks after that my husband lost his job too. It was terrible. I had to keep roomers and boarders. The roomers paid two dollars a week and the boarders paid more because I cooked for them. I had about three of them and that helped pay the rent. There was no welfare in those days. My boarders were boys from Ireland who mostly worked in construction. When they couldn't work they left and went home, some worked their way home on a cattle boat.

Eventually I got a job in the Dominion Square Building cleaning offices six nights a week for ten dollars a week. I was only there a short time when my husband met me one morning—he had been out every morning looking for work. This morning he told me that he had got a steady job working for the City of Montreal and that I could stop working. He was getting seventeen dollars a week cleaning the streets and clearing snow in the wintertime. He happened to know an Irishman, Paddy Scullion, who got him the job. We decided that I'd work for a little while longer until we got on our feet. Then my three children took whooping cough and I had to quit work.

It really was hard in the thirties. A lot of the neighbours had no work. We'd go to the Atwater market on Saturday night after the farmers would leave and take a piece of newspaper. We didn't even have a bag in those days. We'd pick up a piece of turnip if it was lying on the ground, or a carrot, or a cabbage leaf, bring it home, boil it and eat it. We were glad to get it. When I see people living high today I remember what we went through.

All my friends are gone and my two brothers have passed away. I was very close to my youngest brother who stayed in Montreal and his wife and I are still close. I can't speak French though, and that makes living in Quebec hard. Some of the bus drivers are nice but some are terrible. One day a bus driver told me to move to the back but I couldn't because I walk with a cane and I have to hold on to the pole. He kept on yelling at me to move to the back. He wouldn't do that to a teenager. He'd be too afraid, but they pick on old people. I have a lot of very nice French friends, really nice people, but I can't speak the language. I don't go out much because it's nearly all French. I'm also too old to leave at this point.

Sarah Layden at eighty-six. She came to to Montreal
in 1928 just as Canada was heading into the Depression.
"We'd go to the Atwater Market on Saturday night after the
farmers would leave and pick up a piece of turnip if it was
lying on the ground, or a carrot, or a cabbage leaf, bring it
home, boil it and eat it. We were glad to get it."
Courtesty of Sarah Layden.

Cliff Sowery

When contacted for an interview, Cliff Sowery's first reaction was: "Anything I can do for the Irish, I'll do. If you've got an Irishman for a friend, you've got a friend for life. I love the Irish." The Irish community of Griffintown had a very good friend indeed in Cliff Sowery. As the director of the Griffintown Boys' and Girls' Club, he devoted most of his life to the youth of the area. His affection for the Irish was returned by many grateful Griffintowners who will never forget him. He was well known as a boxing instructor and is a member of the Canadian Boxing Hall of Fame. He was born in Wareham, Dorset, England in 1906 and came to Canada with his mother, two sisters and seven brothers around 1912, first settling in St. John, New Brunswick. The family moved to Montreal in 1919.

My mother was a marvellous little woman. She lived to 101. We were all about six feet tall and she was a little thing. We'd get her in the middle like a football play and kid her along. She'd look up at us and say, "I don't give a damn for you buggers." She was a wonderful woman. She did housework, day work, scrubbing schools and things like that and raised eight boys and two girls all by herself. She brought us out here to Canada. I wasn't the best; I ran away from home more times than enough, maybe a dozen times. We moved to Montreal in 1919—one of my sisters was married to Ed Hollett, a fireman here that she met during the war. We lived on Rozel Street in Point St. Charles. It was a wonderful community and there was a great spirit down there. I played lacrosse, hockey and baseball and I used to be the goalkeeper for the Belding Corticelli soccer team. I worked as a mailboy for them and I loved that company. My friends were of all different backgrounds because sports brought us together.

I first went down to the Griffintown Club as a volunteer in 1929. I was supposed to fight in the Forum for the promoter Armand Vincent and I asked a fellow where I could find a good place to train. He was from Griffintown and he told me to go there. Dr. Gibson Craig was the boxing coach at the time, he was also the intercollegiate welterweight champion. I took over when he quit. I developed some of the outstanding fighters of Canada: Johnny Greco, Freddy Daigle, Tony Mancini, Gus Mell and Armand Savoie. I sent four boys to the Olympics. They didn't win but they were the champions of Canada anyway. We fought in the Chicago Stadium, in Detroit and all over. I was at the club until 1956 and I eventually became the director. The club took in everybody regardless of race, colour or nationality. They came from Point St. Charles and from all over. We even had them coming from the West Island. I organized what they called the Junior Golden Gloves. I trained Gus Mell from a little kid of six years of age when he was only a little guy who weighed forty-five pounds. Our smallest trunks looked like a pair of pajamas on him. He made a lot of money out of boxing but he threw it away. It was too bad because he was a classy and colourful fighter. Joe Coughlin was a rugged Irishman who had more courage than he had anything else. He was marvellous and one of the best fighters.

How did I become a boxer? I was in the U.S. Marine Corps. I changed my name and joined under the name Cliff Summers. I was an illegal immigrant because I wasn't allowed at that time to go to the States. I was there from 1930 to 1935. I had done some boxing when I was about sixteen; I used to work out with Jimmy Gill on Charlevoix Street. In the marines they don't ask you if you ever fought before. They come out and ask, "What do you weigh?" You say, "165 pounds." "You're fighting tonight." There was a small stadium which held about 3,000 Marines and they'd match you up with your weight even if you never had a glove on in your life. I got eight Marines together and took them down to the gymnasium and trained them and we won the whole seven bouts. They lifted me up on their shoulders. I was a hero. I was a middleweight—5'11" and 160 pounds and in wonderful shape.

You'll never realize what people went through during the Depression. We built a coffin for this Irish guy when his little three-year-old daughter died and he couldn't afford the twenty-five dollars for the coffin. We stayed up till two o'clock in the morning and made a nice white pine coffin. That was Griffintown. You took part in everything. The people were really proud. They wouldn't ask you for help. You had to find out from somebody else if they were in trouble. It was so bad during the Depression that people burned their shutters and the adjoining doors to keep warm in the winter. I loved the people in Griffintown. They were mostly Irish, a few Welsh and Scottish. They were loyal to the club. You never had to ask for extra help. If you ever wanted help cleaning the gym after the movies for the dance they all got a broom and swept up and put the chairs away and everything else. They were so willing to give you any help you could use.

The O'Donnells, of King's Transfer—there is a wonderful outfit. They saved us thousands of dollars. During the war when we had to transfer our boxing ring around to different armouries or hotels, they did it for nothing. And anytime you wanted any clothes or furniture picked up in Westmount, they used to pick it up and never charged us a cent in all the years we were down there. They were wonderful and they didn't have it themselves. They just had an old Model T van. They also had a wonderful mothers' group down in Griffintown. They raised more money with rummage sales and different things like that all during the war. They sent about 400 cigarettes every month to all the different theatres of war, Libya, England, France and Germany. They sent hundreds of Christmas baskets over every year with playing cards and everything else.

A bomber crashed into Griffintown in 1944.* It was a Ferry Command with a Polish crew. They were taking it across to Europe and they got in a spin and before they realized it they were landing on top of the houses. They couldn't pull out and they crashed. Killed fifteen. I was with Chief Paré who was the director of the Fire Department at that time. We were walking across the ashes and he asked, "Do you think there's anybody else?" I said, "Well, there's a woman right on the corner there where the bomber hit and she should be over here." We were walking across the ashes and suddenly the whole thing collapsed and we were down in ashes up to our chest. He was the chief and it was a good thing for me he was. All the firemen rushed over to pull him out and they pulled me out too. When they dug over by the wall there was the woman. She was black like charcoal leaning over the crib with her two kids in there. They were burnt just like charcoal. It crashed right near the club; in fact, the tail hit the corner of the club and it took out a section of the houses right across the street. Margaret Dowling was in the club looking across to her house with tears coming out of her eyes. The firemen were going in and out, up and down the stairs and suddenly they came down with a stretcher covered over with a black tarpaulin. It was her mother. She had just come home from work and was sleeping. All the bodies covered with tarpaulins were laid down at the garage of the Montreal Light, Heat and Power. It was like a morgue.

The Griffintown Boys' Club had a dental clinic, a well-baby clinic and a pre-natal clinic. We had all sorts of things to look after the people of the district. It was run by the Welfare Federation and Owen Dawson was one of the original founders. He and Dr. Flanagan, "Flin" Flanagan. Flanagan was the rock of Gibraltar and the main driving force. He was a Protestant and a football hero at McGill. He raised money for so many things. I could go to him for anything and he'd go after his friends for the money and he'd get it. He knew all the best people in Montreal and he didn't take no for an answer. He loved the kids in Griffintown and he provided dental services for nothing. We used to supply milk for all the 250 kids coming in every day during the Depression for meals, and all the wives of the directors looked after the cooking and waited on the kids. These were all people from Westmount. In the summer, we used to take the kids up Remembrance Road to the mountain in three special streetcars. We had games

Cliff Sowery training young pugilists in the boxing room
at the Griffintown Club.
From booklet: *The Story of the Griffintown Club,*
Courtesy of William O'Donnell.

Cliff Sowery Night, October 1, 1986. Cliff Sowery with Ian Clyde, one of the many
successful boxers that he trained. Cliff was one of the Griffintown Club's most
devoted and loved workers.
Courtesy of Cliff Sowery.

and crafts and everything else all over the mountain. The priests at St. Ann's were friendly enough but the brothers were the hard ones. They'd ask the kids, "Who was at the Griffintown Club last night?" And if a kid put his hand up he was sent home and he had to come back with his parents. The brothers didn't want the kids to go to the club. I don't know what they thought would happen. When the Sodality [a parish society for women which promoted devotion to the Blessed Virgin] was having a reunion they borrowed all the cups and saucers and cutlery from the club and the chairs too. But other times, they didn't want to have anything to do with us. But when they needed anything....even when St. Ann's wanted to play basketball, they used to borrow our basketball to play. We tried to co-operate with them. We'd run field days and everything else down there. There was no antagonism at all.

We had movies at the club on Friday night. The kids paid a nickel and nobody was ever barred if he didn't have money. It used to be funny sometimes. All the little kids used to come from around St. Antoine and Guy. Little French kids, you know, with their big brown eyes. The kids from Griffintown would say, "They're not members." The French kids would be looking at me. In they went. (laughs) Same with the Christmas parties. The kids all knew who belonged because they were all English-speaking and these were little French kids. I couldn't turn any kid away at all.

After the movie was over, the dance would start. The movies were for the younger kids and the dances would be for the older ones. We had our own orchestra called the Griffintown Group with two saxophones, a violin, piano and drums. I played the piano accordion. In that district you had to be careful. There was a gang with this guy named Hook from the West End. He came down there one night during a dance and somebody told me that he was going to clean out the Griffintown Club. He was downstairs blocking the girls' washroom so I went down. I said, "You come down here looking for trouble. Take your gang and get out right now before you get killed." He said OK and he left. I had to do this myself. I wouldn't back down from anybody. I wouldn't care if it was a whole gang, I was going to take them on anyway. They respected me. They knew I could fight which was a big thing in my favour.

What ruined a lot of people in Griffintown was booze. They couldn't control it. I didn't drink and it was just as well because I had a standing invitation with the National Brewery to go in there and drink when I wanted, anytime I liked. Poverty was the main reason, you know. People worked hard—maybe for a dollar a day, shovelling coal over in Goose Village. That was the thing that caused them to go to booze. Hard work and no money. You had to drown your troubles in some way.

We had a marvellous old Irish cop named Hogan. He was respected by the people. If, say, the husband got drunk, he'd escort him home, take him in and say, "Missus, look after him." Other cops would have arrested him and put him in jail, but he used to take them home.

In 1956 I went to work at the Point St. Charles Club. The Griffintown Club closed and changed its budget over to this new club. I didn't get along with Mr. Wylie of the Point St. Charles Club. Everything that was run down there, I did it, but he said that I wasn't co-operating and he fired me. I didn't even get a pension. It wasn't an eight-hour job; I put in thirteen-fourteen hours a day and I got an awful dirty deal, I thought.

Griffintown is all gone now and the Irish have moved out. They have enhanced the other districts of Montreal like Verdun and the West Island. They were great people. They would take the clothes off their backs to help others. I'd love to do it all over again. It was wonderful. A lot of work and a lot of time but it was worth it. They were happy times.

* This is one tragedy remembered by many Griffintowners. It is certainly a terrifying thing to have a huge aircraft fall out of the sky on a spring day. The bomber, a Consolidated B-24 Liberator, was on its way to Europe heavy with freight when the mainly Polish crew ran into difficulty. The plane crashed in the middle of Griffintown a little after 10:30 a.m. Tuesday, April 25, 1944. The five airmen were killed and it is believed that they were all members of the British Royal Air Force. There was a widespread but unsubstantiated rumour in Griffintown that the plane was carrying a cargo of gold. The headline of the *Gazette* of April 26, 1944 read: 15 Known Dead and 1 Missing in Liberator Crash Here."

In an article about the crash on page one, the *Gazette* continues;

> In the corridors of the club, general manager Cliff Sowery tirelessly answered questions. The club was the nucleus of policemen, firemen, reporters and photographers...

John James (Jake) McConomy

Jake McConomy was born in Point St. Charles in 1906. He came by his interest in politics honestly. His great-grandfather, grandfather and father were all involved in the political life of the area known first as the Village of St. Gabriel and later called Point St. Charles. Jake spent almost forty years at City Hall working for the Department of Public Works. His many friends remember Jake (called The Senator) as a renowned storyteller with a wonderful personality whose eyes would light up as he spoke.

Griffintown and Goose Village (which used to be called Victoriatown) were part of the City of Montreal but Point St. Charles was called the Village of St. Gabriel. In 1905 it was annexed to the City of Montreal as St. Gabriel's Ward. I know this because my great-grandfather was the mayor of the Village of St. Gabriel. My grandfather, my father's father, was the leading alderman who negotiated the annexation and held on for a year until he got a good deal from the City.

As the Ukrainians, Polish and Hungarians started to move into the Point, the Irish were beginning to sell and move out. With the money they got from the sale of their houses, they built property in other areas like N.D.G. This would have been around 1919, the year I started at Loyola. I remember standing with Canon O'Meara, who was the parish priest of St. Gabriel's, when Father Peter Heffernan left by horse and buggy to become the first pastor of St. Augustine's. Canon O'Meara said to me, "He's going way out in the country, boy." (laughs) They had their first Mass in the fire station on Côte St. Antoine Road. Father Peter Heffernan founded the parish and his brother, Father Tom Heffernan, from St. Thomas Aquinas, succeeded him.

My father's name was Joseph Augustus McConomy. He hated the name Augustus so everybody called him Gus except for Doc McGovern, our family doctor, who used to call him Joe. My father used to take me around with him and tell me stories. My wife says, "You'd think you were a hundred years old, the way you talk." (laughs) My grandfather married one of the McKeowns, whose father was mayor and chief magistrate of St. Gabriel's, but my grandfather actually ran the place. In those days they used to arrest the Irish on Saturday night because they wouldn't go home with their pay. They all worked six days a week then. They'd be out drinking so they used to round them all up and bring them down to the station on Island Street. Their wives would come and have them released but they were supposed to appear in court on Monday morning. Monday morning came and McKeown, the judge, would call out, "Denis

McCarthy" or something like that and the answer would be, "He's not here." McKeown would get angry. It was McConomy, his son-in-law, telling him that the person wasn't in court. "Where is he? He's supposed to be here. This is a court.""Well," said McConomy, "it's more important for him to go to work than to come to court." (laughs) So all the charges would be dropped, one after the other.

Another story I heard and will always remember is about the open elections. You went up on stage, gave your name, got your ballot and you voted so they knew how the vote was going all day long. There was one Protestant fellow who was a bookkeeper (today they'd call him an accountant). He was running in an area which had a lot of Irish. These Irish had been farmers in Ireland and had been forbidden to be educated by the English. They didn't have much education and this man ignored them. My grandfather told him that he'd better be careful because if this group turned on him, he'd lose his seat. "They have nobody to take my place," he said.

My grandfather decided to run the village fool against this guy. The fool was beating the hell out of him. (laughs) The parish priest went to my grandfather and said, "Tom, don't make a mess of the whole thing." My grandfather said, "The Protestant guy is not going to lose but he's going to lose up until the last hour, and then he's going to have to apologize to a lot of people that he wouldn't even talk to before." My grandfather built a confectionery business which also did catering for dances and such. Two of my uncles were involved in that business. Another uncle worked for the CPR as a secretary to the vice-president. My father was chief engineer of the waterworks of the City of Montreal.

My grandfather was a Conservative Party organizer. You see, St. Ann's Ward was always Conservative. Monsignor Donnelly was a leading Irish clergyman before Msgr. McShane. He was the pastor of St. Anthony's and was entertained by all the Irish who lived on Dorchester Boulevard like Senator Cloran and the Shaughnessys. He would never interfere in elections except they used to say that the Sunday before election day, Msgr. Donnelly ended his sermon by telling the people, "Remember now, tomorrow is election day and blue is heaven and red is hell." (laughs) When I graduated, Father Donnelly said, "I want to see you Jake. Come and see me." I didn't go to see him but when I told my father he said that I should have gone because he said that Father Donnelly always felt that he owed the McConomys a lot. My father said, "Your grandfather, who was the Conservative organizer for Joe Beaubien (that's the Beaubiens of Outremont today), once helped Father Donnelly's father." Father Donnelly used to go to the

States for his health during the summertime but he always travelled in the southern part where the races were. (laughs) But Conservative or Liberal, the people all helped one another. They used to say to my grandfather, "Tom, he's a Liberal, he's not one of us." My grandfather would answer, "No, he's Irish, he's from the Point and that's good enough for me."

Ropery Street, Grand Trunk Street, Laprairie Street and Chateauguay Street, that was the block in the Point which we used to call the "Kerry Patch." You see, when the Irish came over here, they came from different counties in Ireland and they were very clannish. They were mostly pick and shovel men who were hired out every morning. They were building the CNR at that time and the big foreman was from County Kerry. (I got a lot of these stories from my father, who was around at that time and whose father and grandfather were involved in politics) All the men would line up with their shovels. The foreman would say, "All the men from Kerry, step forward." They would step forward and the foreman would then say, "That's all I need today." (laughs) That's where the Kerry Patch came from because the Kerry men got the jobs and the money to build their houses. They all bought and built close to one another. Some of the families who lived there were: the Healys, (Father Healy's family), the Kennys, (Fathers Jim and John Kenny's family), the Sheehans, the Ryans, the Philipses, the McCarthys, the Egans, (Jack Egan, the lacrosse player, came from there). We used to kid one another. We used to say that if you started taking any of the girls from the Kerry Patch out, their old man would ask to see your bank book. (laughs) Which was true, too! The Reids, (Father Reid's family), the Mullinses and our family built further over in the Point. My father's family was from Donegal and my mother's family was from Clare. The area was mostly all Irish then.

The French lived in St. Henry. Sometimes the French boys would marry the Irish girls in the Point so they would go back and forth from St. Henry to the Point. Many of them got married in the Irish church and stayed in the Point. There was no school or church for the French. My father told me this story: The people of St. Henry were starting to populate the Point and they wanted a French church of their own. They came as a delegation one Sunday afternoon with their families and a priest they had brought from St. Henry and asked the parish priest, Father Salmon to allow them to say Mass in the basement of St. Gabriel's Church. Father Salmon said, "I refuse to allow you to ever say Mass in the basement of the church." They asked why. Father Salmon told them, "If you start saying Mass in the basement of the church, in ten years we'll be downstairs and you'll be upstairs. We have received the land for this church, our school, the presbytery, and housing for the Irish brothers we're going to bring over for our parish. The council of St. Gabriel Village is willing to give you land, enough to build a church, a presbytery, your own school and a house for the brothers for the school." And that's how the two churches were built one alongside the other. Both churches burned down and both were rebuilt. I was there when St. Charles burned down. It was on a June afternoon and most of the Irish were at Otterburn Park for the annual picnic for the juveniles of the parish. The priest rushed in and saved the chalice and the hosts. The French who came to the Point mingled with the Irish and many became proprietors. They certainly developed a wonderful parish, St. Charles. We used to go to parties on Saturday nights and stay all night until it was time to go to church. Then we'd all go to the French church, which had a Mass at half past five in the morning. The churches were very close together and the two pastors were good friends. You'd often see the two of them out walking.

I remember when the French and later on the Polish, the Italians and the Ukrainians used to call my father Mr. Boss. I would go to the door and see a man and his little girl. The man couldn't speak English so the little one, around ten years of age, would be the interpreter. "My father wants to see the Boss." The father would talk to her and she would talk to my father and they'd do business. A lot of the immigrants were in business, owned stores or worked as butchers. All of them, whether they were German, Hungarian or anything else, were called "Polacks" by the Irish. These immigrants were very close and the women were workers. They built a lot of property in Verdun and their kids went to high school. Some of them rented cold-water flats in the Point, say, five or six rooms, for thirteen dollars a month and I can remember once when someone came to see my father to see if he could get an extension on his lease. My father asked him why and he said, "I own property in Verdun but it's too expensive for me to live in. I can live in your flat for thirteen dollars a month and I can rent my property in Verdun for twenty-five dollars a month." (laughs) They raised their kids well and I don't know how the hell they did it. The children had bikes like the rest of us kids and they took music lessons. The old man was maybe a labourer for the Dominion Steel Company and labourers didn't make a hell of a lot of money in those days.

My father worked as the chief engineer of the Waterworks of the City of Montreal. As a kid of nine or ten years of age, I used to go with him on Sundays. He was in charge of the pumping stations and the reservoirs. He was very devoted to his job and Sunday was the same as any other day. My father and I

Jake McConomy was born in Point St. Charles in 1906.
"My mother wouldn't move out of the Point even
though I was going to Loyola College."
Photo courtesy of Richard McConomy.

would walk up to Atwater Avenue, where the water went through, just to have a look and to see how things were going. They used to burn three carloads of coal a day to operate the pumps for the boilers. The labourers were called coal trimmers and many of them were out of work. My father was hiring them at five dollars a day, which was good pay. I remember one time when Mr. Bertrand, the man who lived downstairs and who worked as one of the coal trimmers, came and told my father, "I'm not going to work tomorrow. I quit my job." "Why? Got a new one?" said my father. "No, there's a strike going to be called tomorrow. They want more money." My father told him he didn't have to quit and said that he would handle the strike, if there was one. He also said that the men were damn lucky to be getting five dollars. When the men came off the coal pile the next day, they came across the yard to where the office was and told my father that there was going to be a strike. "Tell the leaders to come in and see me." So they came in and started to have a meeting. Of course they had no union or anything at the time. My father said, "Who's the leader responsible for this?" "It's Mr. So-and-so and Mr. So-and-so." "Well," said my father, "Mr. So-and-so and Mr. So-and-so, you're fired. You're no longer employees. Anybody else who wants to take their place come on up and you'll be fired too. Or else get back to work." And that was the end of the strike.

My mother wouldn't move out of the Point even though I was going to Loyola and my sister was at Marguerite Bourgeois College. My father told her he was going to buy a house on Rushbrooke Street but, at the last minute, when it came time to sign the papers, the guy increased the price a thousand dollars and my father told him to shove it. So we tore down a two-tenement, cold-water flat, leaving the framework up, and rebuilt the house. My mother died about four years later. Life is funny, eh? My mother died suddenly. She was visiting at her mother's one Saturday night. My father went over to meet her and pass the evening. We only lived on the next street over. When they got home, she said to Father, "Well, I'll lay on the chesterfield and read the paper. Tell the boys and the girls to come in." *The Standard* used to come out on Saturday night. She died just like that. She was fifty-two and had everything to live for. My young brother was only about nine years old. We had a new home and in 1922, I think it was, my father had bought another house on the waterfront in Woodlands which is past Chateauguay. My mother's mother lived to be eighty-seven.

I worked at the Montreal City Hall for thirty-seven years. At the end I was chief of staff for the Department of Public Works. I worked for five directors but Lucien L'Allier was the smartest guy, French or English, that I ever worked for. I retired in 1965 on St. Patrick's Day. I walked in and quit in ten minutes. Wrote out my resignation and handed it to the chief. I told him, "I'm the last Irishman to work for the City because you're not hiring any more these day and you never will." He said, "You were here last night until six o'clock." I said, "Just until ten minutes ago, Charlie. I can't take it any longer."You couldn't fire any of the employees. They'd practically have to assault you or something, you know. I remember talking to one guy and he said, "Who do you think I am, your servant?" (laughs) And he was a clerk! And Drapeau was one of the worst. I remember when I gave Robillard (who was a very clever guy and a graduate engineer from McGill), the job of bringing all the forms up to date—the estimate forms, order forms, purchase forms—all the different bilingual forms. I happened to say to Robillard one day, "Where are the forms? How are they advancing?" He told me that he had given them to Mayor Drapeau to look at and that they were at the printer's. I asked to see the copies and saw that they were only in French. He said, "The new ones are only going to be in French. The mayor decided that." That would have been in '55 or '56. That's when it started.

Mayor Camillien Houde was the best organizer I ever saw. At meetings, they used to make Manhattan cocktails and martinis by the jugful. (laughs) All you did was sit there with your glass and this guy kept walking up and down filling it. Then the mayor would begin the meeting by announcing, "Well, I guess you fellows are all ready." He spoke English and French thoughout and there were only two of us English-speaking ones on the committee, the rest were all French. "My Irish friends," he used to say. The city employees would give money to one of the charities. There were three of them, the Catholic charities, the French charities and the Protestant charities. Today they have Centraide. Those who wanted to contribute used to have an employee card which was used to deduct money from their salaries. It was usually a very small percentage of our salary every payday and Mayor Houde would give a big dance in the Hall of Honour for everyone who contributed that way. There would be drawings for prizes, too.

Charles Blickstead

Charles Blickstead, known as Sir Charles to his friends, was born on Duke Street in Griffintown in 1907 and lived there until the family moved away in 1930. At the age of seventeen, he left Montreal to spend a few years in New York City. When he returned, he became a fireman. After about thirteen years or so as a firefighter, he was assigned to start up a training school for firemen which, until that time, did not exist. In 1943-45 he served as a lieutenant-commander in the Royal Canadian Navy. As naval fire marshall, he was its chief instructor. One thing he did not like was the affected British accents adopted by some Canadian naval officers. He retired from the Montreal Fire Department in 1956 but continued on as a consultant until 1982.

I spent all of my childhood and youth in Griffintown and have some very fond memories of that period and of the very fine people that I used to know. I imagine that most of these people have passed on and there aren't too many of us left of that generation. I still go back to Griffintown periodically to look it over again and to bring back memories. While there's not much left of the Griffintown that I used to know, I still recognize the streets and I imagine the people and the places that we used to frequent.

My family? Well, I was the only boy and the second last to be born. I had five sisters and Mother and Dad, of course. We lived on Duke Street, between Wellington and Ottawa. It was a very warm neighbourhood in that everyone knew everyone else and it was very friendly. Very helpful, too—people were very kind when one was sick. The neighbours would always come in and do things for my mother or whoever was sick on the block. The street itself is still there but all the buildings and houses have vanished. One of the last landmarks of Griffintown which was on the corner of Duke and Ottawa was demolished just a couple of years ago, and I'm referring now to Esplin's Box Factory. All of the stores that we used to frequent and patronize, all of the bars; they're all gone too. The church is gone, the schools have gone, the kindergarten is gone. What's left is maybe two or three of the people that I used to know. It is a very sad thing when I go down there and I could cry because I felt very good in Griffintown.

My mother was a Kelly from Quebec City. Her mother was from Waterford and her father was from Kilkenny. It was rather an Irish house although Blickstead is not an Irish name. My dad's family came from Norway and Germany. My father couldn't speak a word of any language but English but my mother, God love her, she had a brogue you could cut with a knife. Her brothers, Jack, Dick and Paddy, all spoke with a brogue even though they were born in Quebec. We were raised by the mother, of course, and in an Irish milieu with the priests and brothers and nuns of St. Ann's. We learned to love things Irish. We felt very Irish and I still do.

My father was a printer. They called them compositors in those days. He worked for the *Gazette* for many years. He learned his trade with Bentley's Printing Shop on Bleury Street many years before I was born. My mother was a typical housewife who brought up the children as were all mothers then in Griffintown. They were housewives and mothers. It was very rare to see a married woman go out to work unless she became a widow and had to do so to support her family. That's the way it was in those days.

The boundaries of Griffintown would be McGill Street on the east, the Lachine Canal on the south, to the north would possibly be Notre Dame Street and to the west would be Guy Street.* The Lachine Canal was the dividing line between Griffintown and Point St. Charles although many people in Point St. Charles belonged to St. Ann's Parish which was the parish then of Griffintown. My own view is that there was an invisible line of demarcation which divided Griffintown. West of Colborne Street, the Irish Catholics were pretty much the main body of the population. If you went east of Colborne, (now, I repeat again, this is an imaginary line,) we became more cosmopolitan in the sense that, while there were many Irish Catholics all the way down, there was a mix of Jewish families and French families, a few Italian families, and numerous Protestants also. There were three Protestant churches in Griffintown: St. Edward's, St. Mark's and I think the other one was St. Andrew's. Three different denominations—this indicates that there were more than just a few Protestants. These churches were to the east of Colborne Street. There was also a Protestant school east of Colborne Street on Ann Street which some people may remember as William Lunn School. The French had a school and a church, both called Ste. Hélène. The French church was originally a roller skating rink on St. Maurice Street which was converted to accommodate the French-speaking population. None of these places exist anymore.

There were all kinds of goats in Griffintown. Now you may wonder why there'd be goats in Griffintown. Well, as far as I can recollect, they were kept by stable owners because it was said that if a disease were to occur the goats would get the disease first but they didn't say whether they would pass the disease on to the horses or not. (laughs) We always wondered about that. In any event, there were a number of goats that would roam up and down the streets. They'd leave the stable yards and away they'd go, free to move anywhere they wanted. Now Pat O'Brien had a stable on Duke Street with a large number of horses and a few goats. Everybody knew them. They'd wander the back lanes and eat the garbage and whatever else they could find. One day there was a commotion created by Mrs. O'Flaherty who declared that, "Somebody's stealing the clothes off my line." Well, Lardy Jasus, it went on and on and became an epidemic. People were claiming that someone was stealing the laundry off the lines until one day who comes down the street but Pat O'Brien's goat and he's got Mrs. Regan's drawers hanging from his horn. That solved the mystery of the stolen laundry! With the departure of the horses, of course, came the departure of the goats.

Once I got lost. I was very, very small and, you know, in those days there were no automobiles, only horse-drawn carts and sleighs in the wintertime. I remember hanging on to the back of a sleigh going down Duke Street and I must have fallen off onto the sidewalk. A man came along and asked where I lived. Now I had been taught by my mother: "If you ever get lost always remember the number of your house. It's 95 Duke Street." I remembered the number and the man took me home. Mother would always kiss us good-bye and she'd say, "Now go down very careful. Stay on the sidewalk. Go to the corner. Always look both ways and mind the harses." We didn't have a harse. We had a tree in the back yard. We had the only tree in Griffintown except for Gallery Square. I remember it was a poplar tree and people used to come from miles around to see the Blickstead tree even though there was nothing on it that you could claim.

One of the things I remember so well on Duke Street, and it occurred also on other streets, was that in the summertime (the houses in those days were not insulated against the heat) all the chairs would come out every evening and would be lined up on the sidewalk. All the way down the street you'd see all the neighbours sitting out rocking in the chairs, talking and laughing. It was such a lovely thing to remember. That's gone now. Some of the people would go to Chateauguay in the summer—we called it "Shadagee"—and a lot of people had summer homes out there. My uncles, Paddy and Dick, had a summer house there and so did my Uncle Clarence. People would go for the summer or they'd spend weekends there.

I went to St. Ann's Boys' School for God knows how many years and my sisters all attended St. Ann's Girls' Academy on McCord Street. There weren't any high schools in Griffintown in those days. My recollection of the teachers at St. Ann's Boys' School are all good. They were Christian Brothers, many of them Irish from Ireland and they were not pushovers. Some of them were quite physical. If you did any wrong, you were punished for it but always because you deserved it. I received the strap on many occasions and I look back now and say that I deserved it. But they were great people. After school was over, about three o'clock or three-thirty, few of the boys would go home. Most would hang around the school because the brothers would come out and play hockey. They would hook up their soutanes and stick them under their belts to skate. They were rough and they'd knock you down. They also played football with us and were devoted teachers.

Griffintown was an enclave and at the centre of social activities was the church and St. Ann's Hall. The priests were great in keeping the families together. There was always the annual visitation to the homes and I remember when one of the priests converted the back of the gymnasium to a bowling alley to get the families to bowl together. The priests' house, which was very big, was behind the church. The Redemptorist Fathers were really great priests. They were the ultimate according to my values and my standards. We certainly respected them because they merited the respect. They were great workers and most of them died young because they were overworked. They visited families constantly. The one priest that stands out most of all in St. Ann's when I was a boy and a young man was Father Mylett, an Irishman from Quebec City. But all the priests were great. They also had lay brothers. There was Brother Reginald who was at the desk at the priests' house when people would come in looking for advice and things like that. He also handled the books. Brother Leonard did the menial work, cooking and things like that. The priests took a very great interest in the parishioners. In those days, the priest would go down the street carrying Holy Communion, an altar boy in front of him. When he got to your house, you had the table ready with the candles lit and the crucifix and everything there and a little dish for him to wash his hands. There was a great deal of dignity and respect. I remember Father Mylett getting up in the pulpit one Sunday and he was talking about visiting the sick. He said, "And, another thing, the next time I go into your houses I don't want to see the candle stuck in a whiskey bottle." Ah, they were great. In those days you didn't touch the Host. Any snotty-nosed kid today can carry the vessels anywhere. Today, you don't even have to go to Confession. I went into the confessional one day up in my parish and the vacuum cleaner fell out. (laughs)

Thomas O'Connell, Dan Gallery, John Gallery, Frank Hanley, Tom Healy were some of the leaders in the community. They were very much our people. They were of us and we were of them. There was no protocol necessary. You

(top) In the fall of 1930 Charles Blickstead (left, in the driver's seat) was transferred to Station 10. The men are wearing their winter uniforms. Note the lack of windshields on the trucks.

(bottom) Ready for action at Station 15, 1930.

Photo by D. Pachetty.

Photos courtesy of Charles Blickstead.

could meet them in the street and there was no snobbery.

Electricity came in maybe in 1914, 1915, something like that. When I was a small boy we did not have electricity in the house. We had coal oil lamps and I remember my mother and her sister sitting at the kitchen table trying to read the print in the paper. The paper was *The Witness* or *The Herald* in those days. The coal oil would be delivered to your house once a week by "Coal Oil" McCarthy. He'd go up and down the street ringing the bell, "coal oil, coal oil, coal oil." You'd get your can and he'd fill it. He had a horse and cart with two barrels of coal oil on it. There was an awful lot of stuff delivered to your house by peddlers. There were vegetable peddlers; the milkman would come in the morning with the milk which was served out by the quart or the gallon as you wanted it; the bread and vegetables the same way. I remember old Rafferty used to come. He'd be sick and drunk half the time. You could smell him a mile away and he'd knock on the door and my mother would say, "There's old Rafferty. He's drunk again and here with his frozen fruit." He'd have all his vegetables in this little cart in the wintertime and an old blanket thrown over them. Half the stuff was frozen, you know. These were all the characters. All great people.

Oh, and I remember the man who used to go around lighting the street lights by hand. The boys would come along and put them out again. He was hired by the City, by the Light, Heat and Power Company at that time. He'd light up those gas lamps. That was your street lighting at that time. He'd come back to put them out. We didn't know any better. That's the way it was. And the wooden sidewalks. I remember Dupré Lane had wooden sidewalks. There was a building there which was taken over by Sterling Blend Tea. That would also be delivered to your door by horse and wagon. Prior to Sterling Tea, that building was owned and run by a society called the Young Irishmen.

A common thing at Christmas was to use small special candles which you would light and, in too many instances, trees took fire and people were hurt. I remember fishing around in one of the big cases in the attic of the house and finding candles which had been lit at one time. I don't remember seeing a tree with candles on it because of the fear of fire so we didn't have that. Christmas Eve, you always hung up your stocking along a shelf in the kitchen and in the morning we always had gifts. Oranges and candies and maybe twenty-five cents. I was always active in the Midnight Mass because I was an altar boy and belonged to the choir. Professor McCaffrey was the organist and a little later on my own sister, who was a very fine musician, became the organist and she was there for maybe thirty or forty years. We always had a huge turkey and a huge ham. You could have your choice or have both if you wanted to. I remember my mother slaving over the kitchen stove Christmas Day cooking the ham and the turkey and the big pudding—plum pudding with suet in it and lots of fruit. We would get up from the table and all of us could hardly walk. There was always plenty to eat in the house.

Griffintown consisted of very old houses and the plumbing left something to be desired. For example, there were no bathtubs in the houses unless you bought one and you stuck it in and you had to fill it up with buckets of water. Shortly before I was born, toilet facilities consisted of an outhouse in the back. You would have one sink in the kitchen with a single cold-water tap. Very small kids normally bathed in the washtub in the kitchen but there were public baths throughout the area. You could go to Hushion's Bath or O'Connell's Bath on Haymarket Square or Gallery's Bath and have your shower which most people did. They also had pools, of course, where you could swim. You'd go to O'Connell's and when your half hour or so was up then old Jack McHugh would go around with a stick banging the columns. Bang, Bang, Bang, Bang. "Everybody out." You had to get out, change and go so we'd go from O'Connell's Bath over to Gallery's Bath on the canal bank at Gallery Square and we'd swim there until Johnny Kemp would bang with his stick, "All you, out." Then we had no place to go so we'd go swim in the Lachine Canal. We didn't know anything about pollution. That wasn't invented in those days. There were industries all along the bank and they dumped all their sewage into the canal and there were a lot of ships going up and down but we were kids. We didn't know any better.

There was no refrigeration when we were children. The ice used to be cut off the river and dragged in by two horses drawing sleds loaded with big chunks of ice. Big blocks, oh, maybe five-six feet long by three feet wide and two feet thick. I remember vividly, as a boy, hanging on to the back of these sleds. The horses used to go way out on the river and the men would be out there cutting with a saw. They'd load these sleds and then bring the ice to the ice houses. There were two storage houses on Duke Street, City Ice and Dan Donnelly's. They were huge big sheds. Insulated, you know, and they'd store all this block ice. Come springtime it would be cut up into squares, maybe a foot square, and sold from door to door. It cost ten cents a block. Well, you got your money's worth if you got the ice at eight o'clock in the morning but if the iceman happened to get there at five o'clock in the evening, you weren't getting very much of a piece of ice and they'd charge you the same price. Mother never had an account anywhere. She always had the dime waiting for Jimmy Stacey coming with the block of ice. We had the cleanest hallway in Griffintown. Mother would say, "Jimmy Stacey's coming with the ice. Put the papers down." The newspapers would be spread down the hallway because she had just washed the floor on her hands and knees. "Put down the papers," she'd say and Jimmy would come in with the ice and drip, drip, drip down the hall but it didn't matter and into the icebox it would go, colour and all. I never saw such colourful ice in all my life. It would be brown and pink and all kinds of colours because in those days they didn't have any sewage systems. That's a fact. (laughs) That would go into your icebox with a plunk. No wonder there was so much typhus fever going around.

St. Patrick's Day was always something very special in Griffintown. Many families owned work horses. They'd be hitched to carts and wagons and they'd be used to haul all sorts of things. Very often they would be hired by the City for street cleaning, snow removal and all that sort of thing. They were all work horses until St. Patrick's Day. Some of them were nice looking animals and others were not so nice looking. Regardless, on St. Patrick's Day the horses would be trotted out and one of the young sons would be the jockey. The horse would be bedecked in all kinds of green and white rosettes and the jockeys would be dressed in beautiful emerald green. They'd race up and down Ottawa Street before taking part in the parade. They'd go up and down St. Catherine Street or Sherbrooke Street and scare the daylights out of so many people that it was abolished. St. Ann's Young Men's Society was always very prominent and I remember they all wore the silk hats—what they used to call the stovepipe hats—and all loaded down with shamrocks. They were a fine-looking band of young men. The priests always attended, of course, and the boys from the school. The school was always shut down for the day. There were very few things that would cause you to be expelled from school, and one of them would be not to show up for the St. Patrick's Day Parade.

Family celebrations were usually at home because there were very few, if any, really affluent people in Griffintown. Maybe the O'Connells, the Gallerys, the O'Sullivans and a few like that, the business people. So there weren't too many people who could afford to go out and have a meal in the hotel because most of the families were large. When they did go out for a meal, they went mostly to the Queen's which was on Windsor Street near St. James.

The Arrawanna Club was on Bridge Street just below Wellington. It was a place where you could go when all the pubs were closed or on Sundays. If you wanted a drink, a bottle of beer or anything, you went there. There were many pubs in Griffintown. We called them saloons in those days and my own father was a patron at times but he never overdid it. I remember sneaking under the doors of Paddy Carroll's and saying, "Is my father in there?" Paddy Carroll's was on the corner of Duke and Wellington and, in the summertime when the doors would be open—they had these small swinging doors so you couldn't see in—you'd pass and you'd think it was an airplane with everyone talking at once. That was Paddy Carroll's. Now you'd go to the next corner and it was MacNiece's. It was called a union house. One block further north you'd find on one corner Paddy O'Connell's saloon and opposite him Mike Murphy's Saloon. Then at the corner of St. Paul and Dupré Lane, I think the name was Hennessey's Saloon. People would be there sometimes during the daytime and, of course, the working people would drop in for a snort on their way home. In most cases they went home but there were cases where they didn't want to leave. We used to joke that there was always a brawl going on and you'd have to keep away from the swinging doors because the guys would come flying out the door still sitting on the chair. (laughs) They'd always settle the brawls outside the bars because they'd throw them out and they'd finish on the street. In those days there were no Liquor Commission stores—you bought your booze right there on the counter or it was served to you neat. They'd stand up at the bar and it was a sign of manhood if you could drink the other guy under the table. However, if you left your salary with the innkeeper, the kids couldn't eat for the next week.

I don't think the police were necessary in Griffintown, to tell you the truth, although there were some Irishmen and people of other nationalities too, who were rambunctious at times, but it was largely a peace-loving family area. Sometimes the odd guy would kick over the traces and maybe have too much to drink. By and large there were no robberies. One of my sisters worked for the CPR Telegraph and she came home every night at midnight. She'd walk down from St. Francis Xavier Street through Griffintown in the pitch black. Never once in her lifetime was she molested or accosted or insulted by anybody. And I remember very well the girls that crossed the Haymarket at night. Nobody ever said a word to them, they were always respected.

The Haymarket was a big, bald square. No grass on it, just a square, bounded by William, St. Paul, Duke, and Inspector streets. That's where you bought your hay. Farmers would bring in a ton or two of hay with horse-drawn ricks and they'd spend the day there twice a week. If you owned horses you went to the Haymarket and bought your load of hay. The scale was there for weighing and they'd bring the hay right down to your stable. Every Sunday in the summertime was baseball day in the Haymarket—St. Ann's baseball club and the Emmetts and the Shannons from St. Anthony's. A lot of teams would play there and that would draw quite a crowd of people. They had benches along the sides and that was always a big day in Griffintown on a summer's Sunday.

If you didn't go to the Haymarket then you went to shoot the rapids. You'd take the *Rapids King* down at Victoria Pier. They'd sail up the river and come back down by Lachine. There was a special guide who would take the wheel coming down through the rapids. These were big wooden ships and it was quite a thrill, believe me, because the rapids were rough in those days.

I always wanted to be a fireman. I don't know where I got the bug. I remember as a small boy walking by Station No. 3 on the corner of Dalhousie and Wellington and I remember once seeing eight horses galloping by Duke Street while the firemen were putting on their coats and hats and I used to find that so romantic. My father had other ambitions for me and he was very, very put out when I decided I'd leave school a little bit earlier than normal. He said, "I want you to go to Loyola and become a lawyer." The whole thing, you know. So I said, "I don't want to be a lawyer. I want to be a fireman." I did become a fireman and was one most of my lifetime. I'm the happiest guy in the world that I became a fireman because I loved it. When I joined in 1929 every fire station from, let's say, Bleury Street west was captained by an Irishman. Number 25 and No. 5 were captained by Irish Canadians. So was No. 10, maybe fifteen stations with Irish captains. Christopher Carson was the fire chief at one time and he was from Northern Ireland. The first station to which I was assigned, this was in 1929, still had horses drawing the fire apparatus. This was Station No. 15 in Point St. Charles. Number 9 had horses. The stations downtown had one horse-drawn apparatus and, say, the ladder truck and the pumper would be a motorized vehicle. Gradually, by 1931-1932 all the horses had disappeared in the fire department. I used to be in charge of funerals. I drilled the firemen and led the fireman's band which played at all the firemen's funerals. There'd always be a turnout of men in uniform marching behind the hearse or in front of it. We had a great choir which would sing at weddings and funerals.

Some of the funerals that I remember were lavish affairs. You'd see the hearse coming down driven by two jet-black horses and a beautiful, big glass box. The wheels would be shiny and everything was black. The horses had plumes on their heads, you know, and the guy who was driving would be in uniform with a big top hat or a plume. Wintertime he'd have a fur cape and a big fur hat. It was something beautiful to see. People used to die to get into that hearse just to ride in it. (laughs) And, you know, in those days you used to walk behind the hearse but today they don't do that. When the hearse would leave there would be a cortege, could be ten or a hundred people marching two by two behind it all the way to the church and from the church for a few blocks on the way to the cemetery.

Living in Griffintown eventually became a chore for the people. The new generation wouldn't put up with the old houses. They got the education and the better jobs and saw how other people lived. Verdun and N.D.G were developing, St Michael's Parish, too. The younger generation moved to better themselves socially (maybe that's an imaginary thing) and the girls wanted their boyfriends to come to a more modern house because some of the houses were falling apart. When I married, I lived in Côte St. Paul and when we saved enough money we bought a house in N.D.G. It took us seven years but I moved to N.D.G for one particular reason—to get my kids close to Loyola. A lot of people did the same thing.

The other day when I was passing Gallery Square I noticed that all the swings, the see-saws and the slides are still there and the grass is still being cut. I don't know why. My guess is that they're expecting the kids to come back but they're not coming back. They're all dead but the park is still being maintained.

*These are traditionally considered the boundaries of Griffintown but John Loye, a historian of the Irish community of Montreal wrote the following: "I can state that it was that section of the city, bounded on the east by McGill Street, on the north by St. Maurice, Chaboillez Square, and Notre Dame, on the west by McCord, down to William, and by the latter street westward to Guy. On the south it was bounded by the Lachine Canal." *Source:* John Loye, "A Lost Town," the *Gazette*, November 17, 1936.

Sybil Brown Morse

Sybil Brown Morse was put into the St. Patrick's Orphanage when her beloved mother was killed in a tragic accident in Griffintown. It was an unhappy time in her life and decades later her voice still betrays her strong negative feelings about the experience. Her resentment extends to her father whom she referred to as Walter throughout the interview. A tall, strikingly handsome woman exuding charm and spirit, she lived happily with her widowed daughter in St. Bruno until her death in 2003. One of her granddaughters is Cynthia Coull, one of Canada's finest figure skaters in the 1980s, who has an arena named after her in Greenfield Park.

My mother was Annie Burns. She was born in Montreal as far as I know. My father was Walter Patrick Brown—he wasn't from Ireland. Ireland wouldn't own him. (laughs) He was Scotch and his father was in the Black Watch.

I was born in 1907 in St. Mary's Parish. I don't remember those early years. Later we moved to Barré St. in Griffintown. I went to St. Ann's School and made my First Communion in St. Ann's Church. I left Griffintown when I was about ten years old. Walter put all of us—I had two sisters, Hazel and Beryl—into St. Patrick's Orphanage. My mother was killed on Feb. 14, 1918. I'll never forget it. She was walking along Notre Dame Street on St. Valentine's Day pushing a baby carriage. Her sister was with her and Hazel was in the carriage. She was going to deliver some Valentine cards. She passed a store and some ice fell off the roof and hit her on the head. She would have been thirty years old the next month. The owner had been warned about the ice and Walter got the huge sum of $1,900. His share was $900 and the rest was divided up among us. We were supposed to get it when we were twenty-one. When I tried to get it I had seven dollars. That's what was in the bank. Walter had blown every bit of it. I always said that the wrong person died. My mother could sew. She would have supported us. If my mother hadn't known how to sew we would have seen more dinner hours than dinners.

The orphanage was run by the Grey Nuns. The dormitory was huge with windows all over. There were about sixty-five girls in it and then there were the baby girls. That's where Hazel was and I don't know how they were treated but I know we had one or two nuns there who were beasts. The kids used to be scared stiff to wet the bed because in the morning it meant a cold bath, winter or summer and your sheets went in too. I think it was terrible the way those kids were treated. I was lucky. I didn't wet the bed but my sister did. Some kids never got any sleep because the others would feel sorry for them and they'd wake them up to go to the bathroom. And that kid wouldn't be gone when another one would wake up in a daze and go over to another kid and say, "Go on. Get up."

We wore our own clothes and we all had jobs. Some worked in the laundry and others in the church. You had a whisk and you had to sweep the steps or clean out the candle holders. The part I didn't like was getting the incense ready for Benediction. To this day I can't stand incense. I used to keep my fingers crossed that someone would give me a job in the kitchen because the nun there was a pet. I used to get all kinds of extras from her. She would see to it that I had what was left over from the nuns. There was another nice nun, Sister Veronica. She didn't stay with us. When it was time to take her final vows she went down to the Grey Nuns on Guy Street and she never took her vows. Beryl had the job of washing the dishes. There was a tin underneath the pan that was sharp around the edges and she ended up with every one of her fingers, right up until she died, they were like you took a knife and cut them.

We went to school in the orphanage. Half of the school was girls and half was boys. The Grey Nuns also ran the boys' side. I had an aunt, my mother's sister who used to visit us. I wanted to show her a mark where I was hit with a switch but the nun made sure I wore long sleeves so she wouldn't see it. The nun was beside me and I dared not say too much. She'd pinch the arm off you. You didn't talk about it. Anyway, they would say you deserved it. I just have a bad taste in my mouth about those people. How do I feel about religion? To hell with it. But you don't lose your faith. We were abused, I'd say. We didn't have to go in there. My mother's sister could have looked after us. She wanted to but Walter thought it was a lot easier to put us in St. Patrick's.

The food was awful. Friday was my worst day. Oh God! We started off with barley soup which I couldn't stand then. I'd have it shoved down my throat until I would throw up. Then the whitefish followed and then tapioca pudding. Three things I hated. We had a little smock with a pocket where you could put your hanky. That's where my fish went until I could get outside and dump it. I guess the nuns were on a budget. Maybe if they had more it might have improved conditions. I don't know.

We had to go to Mass every day and I would pass out because I couldn't stand the incense and because you never got breakfast until an hour or two later and I guess I was a hungry kid. I used to get my throat painted every morning with iodine. No wonder I have this deep voice today.

The chaplain of the orphanage was Father Martin Reid. He was from the Point, I think. He was very good to kids. He'd play games with us. If we were playing jacks and ball he'd play too and he'd kick the ball around with the boys. I'd say Father Reid was all right.

At fourteen years of age you had to leave. I didn't know what I was going to do or where I was going to stay. I stayed with one of my father's sisters for a while and when Hazel and Beryl came out Walter took a house. We laugh now but it is true, Walter didn't pay rent. It was easier to move than to pay rent. We lived on Lusignan for a while. I couldn't keep up with Walter and houses. We moved a lot. I can't say that I made friends here or there because we didn't stay long enough to meet people. Since then, I never move. Audrey and I have been in the same house for many years. It affects you. You don't want to bother with that moving bit.

Before I got married I lived in a boarding house in the Point that was run by Mrs. Hastings. I was working at the Northern Electric. She had a big house and she had nineteen fellows and six girls. A lot of people knew that lady, especially from the Northern. I had fun when I was there.

My husband was from the West End. He was very English. His name was Frank Edwin Morse. He came to Canada when he was four years old. I met him when I was staying with a friend on Eleanor Street. Her husband and Frank had gone to a political rally that they had before an election in Griffintown. Thomas O'Connell had all sorts of slogans. He was really giving it to the people, saying they had better vote for him or they'd be eating snowballs that winter.

During the Depression everybody was in the same boat. My husband usually had work. When there was absolutely nothing he had nothing either and then you went on good old relief. You hoped you weren't going to be on it long and get something else. Relief was six dollars a week.

After my experience in St. Patrick's I would say never put a kid in an orphanage although it can get rather sticky living with relatives especially if they have kids. I would also say save a buck and then you won't have to ask anyone for anything. Your buck is your best friend, I'd say.

Norman Carson

Norman Carson is the son of Christopher Carson, an Irish immigrant from the north of Ireland who rose to the top rank in the Montreal Fire Department. Christopher Carson was involved in putting out some of the worst fires in Montreal history such as the Laurier Palace fire, the Cymbeline explosion and the Laurier Garage fire. It was the custom, in the early days, for fire captains to live in the station with their families. Norman Carson had a successful career in business and neither he nor his three brothers followed in their father's footsteps.

We were living in No. 13 Fire Station on St. Catherine Street East when I was born on February 1,1908. I was the first person to be baptized in St. Aloysius Church on February 12, 1908. My father, Christopher Carson was a Protestant from Northern Ireland who came here because he wanted to go out West to farm. When he reached Montreal, he thought he was far enough away from home (laughs) and with not too much money in his pocket he decided to stay here for a while. He applied for a position in the Fire Department and was taken on immediately. After working at it for a few years he decided he liked it.

We were four boys and two girls. My mother was Catholic but my father was the one who insisted (if he was home on Sunday) that if we were going to church, "Get there on time!" He worked twenty-four hours a day all his life. He was only home, I think it was, one afternoon or one day a week. My mother got accustomed to this life. After all, she had lived in a fire station for many years. My father was appointed fire director in 1933. First he was a lieutenant, a captain, a district chief and then a deputy chief before the next step of becoming the director. He was in all the large fires in Montreal. He started out in No. 1 Fire Station down in Youville Square. When he became captain he was in No. 13 in the east end. We moved from the east end to Point St. Charles when he became district chief. We were in Point St. Charles for about nine years and while we were living there he was appointed deputy chief. We moved up to Maplewood Avenue and he worked out of a station between Decelles and Côte-des-Neiges. I don't recall the number now. The city was divided into two halves. There was a French-speaking deputy chief for the east end of the city which started at St. Lawrence Main and went east and my father was the deputy chief for the west end of the city. He spoke only a little French.

My father never, ever fought a fire from outside the building. He walked right into the building as soon as he got there and you didn't see him again until the fire was over. He was injured several times. The worst accident was the Laurier Garage fire when he was director.* He walked right into the garage—the fire was in the back and the odour of gas was very strong. He ordered the firemen out of the garage immediately and, as he turned around to go out, he got as far as the front door when the building just blew up. He was blown out into the centre of the street on Laurier Avenue. Some of the bricks fell on him and one fractured his skull although he never lost consciousness. He broke his arm, lacerated his face and tore his ear in two. He was out of the hospital and back at work in a little over three months. Mr. Paré, who was the chief engineer for the Fire Department created a trophy which was presented to him from the firemen and fire chiefs of the city.

There was the terrible Laurier Theatre fire in the east end of the city. My father was at home on that night and he was called down to the scene of the fire. When he arrived the children upstairs were just piled up one on top of the other. There were ninety-seven children, I think, that died in that fire.** That was the only time I saw him break down after he got home. He seemed to get over these things quickly or maybe he was too busy to think of them afterwards. He was deputy chief when the *Cymbeline* disaster happened at Canadian Vickers.*** Chief Gauthier, the director of the Montreal Fire Department at the time, was on board the ship. There was an explosion which blew Director Gauthier into the water. He was drowned and they didn't find him for about a week or more. There were several firemen and Vicker's workers who were killed in that explosion. Now Marin, who was the deputy chief for the east end had retired but they hadn't replaced him so the only deputy chief was my father. He had to go down there and he went on board ship as soon as he got there. The firemen hesitated but once he got on the gangplank and went in and told them to come on, they followed him and they put the fire out. With Director Gauthier's death, my father became the acting director for all the City of Montreal for a period of two years. (laughs) He stuck it out till the end and refused to retire. There was a request from an alderman that he retire but he said that he hadn't joined the Fire Department to retire when he should be appointed director. He was the last English-speaking fire director and I don't think for fifty years before him there had been another one. The City Council did the same thing in every case with the Police Department and they wanted to do the same with the Fire Department. The English ones were told, "We'll give you full pension if you retire now." (instead of becoming director) They all took their full pension and retired. My father wouldn't take his pension. Maybe you shouldn't put this down but everyone knows it. It was in the *Gazette* and everywhere. They called him down to a meeting of the city council and they said: "About your resignation,

Chief." He said: "Gentlemen, if this is all you have to discuss with me, good afternoon," and he turned around and walked out.

When the Sarah Maxwell School down in the east end caught fire Sarah Maxwell herself handed the children out the window to my father and he passed them down to Presseau, who later became district chief. My father told her to come out and not get any more children but she said, "Oh, there are a few more." The building crashed and although my father had a hold of Sarah Maxwell's dress he could not get a firm grip and she died in the fire.

When my father became district chief, the family lived on Wellington Street in Point St. Charles and he lived in the fire station on Hibernia. He was only off one night and one day a week. He had a little red sleigh with two lovely horses. We used to ride in it and it was wonderful. The station was a good-sized building. He had an office and a bedroom, each about the size of an average dining room. There was also a bathroom with a shower and bath. The captain had a bedroom on the opposite side of the building and the lieutenant had one at the back of the building. There was a spare room where they could play cards or meet and talk. Downstairs there was a great big room the whole size of my six-room duplex here and the beds were lined up one after the other along each side. There were usually about four men on each apparatus and two to three apparatuses so that would indicate there were twelve or fifteen beds lined up on each side of this room. They slept with their shirts on and their rubber boots beside the bed. Their pants were stretched out on the floor so the minute they put their feet out of the bed they just yanked on their pants and stepped into their rubber boots. Then they went to the pole and down. The firemen had to keep the station absolutely neat and clean. They were always polishing the apparatus and drying the hoses. There were always things to do like keeping the horses clean and fed. The horses were lined up in stalls in the back. My father was captain when the first truck was placed in No. 20 Fire Station on Craig Street. There was a booth on the ground floor in which there was always a fireman on duty. There was also the bell which rang on all three floors but the man on the ground floor had to write the number that came in, where it was and do a full report. If a second alarm came in that would mean that some of them would have to move out of that station and move to another to be more central to the area. A third alarm and again they might have to move to another station where they wouldn't sleep. They were up for the night then. From time to time, there would be friction but the firemen settled things themselves. Of course, they weren't allowed to gamble but there were times...My father was on the top floor and

A young Norman Carson (sporting a cast on his left wrist) with his
parents. "My father was one of the first non-Catholics to be buried in
Côte-des-Neiges Cemetery."
Courtesy of Norman Carson.

he'd come walking down the stairs and there'd be six or seven of them at a table playing poker. He'd walk over and say, "Oh, playing poker? Deal me in a hand." He'd reach over and take some chips from every one of them. Of course, he'd ruined their game. (laughs) They were ready to murder him but this was his way of doing things.

Although my father had to live in the station, he could always drive home for lunch or supper and drive back again because we lived very close to the station. I used to go there to see him. I don't think my father wanted my brothers or me to become firemen. Rae and Harold went to Loyola College. Rae became a dentist and Harold was a chemist. He later became the manager of the Lipton Soup Company. Jim was in the customs business and I was president of the Canada West Indies Molasses Company. I started as a shipper and took some night courses in accounting. I was an accountant from about 1936 to 1952. I became vice-president and then in 1952 I became president. My sister Vivian was a dental nurse and married a dentist, Dr. Barr. Lorraine stayed at home and drove my mother wherever she had to go.

I was living at home and working for a stock brokerage. I was doing quite well but they laid me off during the Depression because my father had what they considered a good job. I didn't exactly like it. I was out, I guess, for a couple of years. They didn't lay me off right at the beginning. They kept you as long as they could hoping the Depression would end. Meanwhile the Molasses Company was expanding. They were putting up new tanks and they wanted another boy. I applied and got the job. During the war, all our ships were taken over by the Admiralty in London because they were all under British flag and we weren't getting supplies. They arranged a job for me with DIL (Defence Industries Limited) at the head office in the Birks Building right at Philip's Square. Then I transferred out to Canadian Vickers where I became chief accountant. I stayed there until they turned the company over to Canadair. When that was done my own company wanted me back. During the war I also joined the Home Guard (laughs) and we had a training camp in St. Bruno.

My father was asked to be the grand marshall of the St. Patrick's Day Parade and he accepted it. I'd say it was in 1933 or 1934. He had just been appointed director. I think he enjoyed it up to a point. There were a few people watching the parade who shouted things like, "What's a Protestant doing in the parade?" It was just the odd spectator, not a general thing.

My father kept up his Protestant faith. He suffered a stroke in the Protestant church and was taken to St. Mary's Hospital where he died six or seven days later. He was eighty-five when he passed away and my mother was sixty-nine, I believe, when she died. My father was one of the first non-Catholics to be buried in Côte-des-Neiges Cemetery. I think Rae arranged that somehow.

* On June 26, 1938, the *Gazette* quoted Fire Captain Napoléon Dugal about this fire: " I was looking around to see if there was any more fire coming up from the basement when the explosion came. All my men and I were thrown through the front of the building as bricks and debris crashed on our heads. I found myself lying in the street. Some of the men must have been badly injured. They were lying all around me."The garage was on Laurier Ave. near Hutchison Street. Three firemen were feared dead and more than one hundred people were injured. Fire Director Carson was among the most seriously hurt while directing operations just inside the garage.

** The *Gazette* of Jan. 10, 1927 reported that seventy-six children had died but the actual number was seventy-eight.There was a stampede which followed a minor fire. The Laurier Palace was at 1683-5 St. Catherine Street East. It was after this disaster that Quebec enforced a regulation barring children younger than sixteen from movie theatres.

*** The Cymbeline's fuel oil was ignited while the ship was being repaired. The explosions killed twenty-seven and another thirty-seven people were sent to hospitals. Director Raoul Gathier and three firefighters were among the dead.

Sister Margaret Power, R.S.C.J.

Sister Margaret Power was born and educated in Montreal. She entered the religious life and spent many years as a Sacred Heart educator in schools both here in Canada and in the United States. At the age of sixty-five she became a social activist and moved with two other nuns to Little Burgundy and began working with welfare recipients. Sister Power was the recipient of the Bishop Crowley Award in 1987 for her many years of work as a welfare advocate with ODAS (Organisation d'aide aux Assistés Sociaux).

I was born on May 16, 1908 in Montreal. We lived on McGill College Avenue and belonged to St. Patrick's Parish. My father was the manager of the City and District Savings Bank on the corner of McGill College and St. Catherine. It was a new branch when he was sent to it and as manager he had a two-storey apartment on top of the bank so that's where we lived. Later we moved to Kensington Avenue in Westmount, but I was already at McGill so I lived most of my early life on McGill College Avenue. I was one of seven children. We were four girls and three boys. I had an older sister, Ruth, who was born exactly one year before I was. She died when she was thirty-three years old. She was walking on the sidewalk and a car drove up on the sidewalk and killed her.

All my grandparents were Irish. The Powers came from Wexford and Waterford and we were always so proud that my mother's family was related to Cardinal Vaughan from Tipperary. My grandfather Power lived on Coursol Street and owned another property on Murray in Griffintown which my father inherited.

My mother used to go to Mass every day. My father didn't but he was the most charitable man I've ever known in my life. I don't mean in the sense of almsgiving although he did his share of that; I mean in his attitude to people and the way he talked. He never criticized or put people down. He was always supportive and neither of my parents would impose anything on us. They never said that we should become nuns. I remember when we all had the flu in 1918 except my mother and father. Billy was only three years old and he had double pneumonia as well. Father Singleton from St. Patrick's came to bless him because they thought he was going to die. I was ten years old but I still remember my mother coming to me while I was sick in bed and asking me to pray that Billy would be cured and that if he were cured that he would become a priest. That's the kind of faith that we had and absorbed. When he got better, he had to learn to walk all over again. He did become a priest and he knew that that was what he wanted from the time he was twelve years old. My mother never said, "Oh,

(Left to right) Sister Mary Power, R.S.C.J., Kevin Power,
Sister Margaret Power, R.S.C.J., Walter Power,
Sister Elizabeth Power, R.S.C.J., and
Bishop William Power. This extraordinary family
gathered together to celebrate Sister Margaret Power`s
Golden Jubilee, August 6, 1990 at Sacred Heart
School in Montreal.
Courtesy of Sister Margaret Power.

we have to have a priest in the family."There was none of that. The same with us. There was no pressure about becoming nuns.

I went to elementary school at St. Patrick's Academy which was on St. Alexander Street right opposite the church. We were taught by the CND nuns. My sisters and I went to the Sacred Heart Convent which, at that time, was also on St. Alexander. The convent was a bilingual school. The English girls and the French girls were in separate classes but we mixed together for dinner, recess, sewing class and singing and I made friends with many of the French girls. My brothers Walter and Billy started at St. Patrick's School for Boys and then Walter went to Loyola. Billy went to the Collège de Montréal. By the time Kevin went to school we had moved to Kensington and so he went to St. Leo's and later to McGill.

When it was time for me to go to college I decided to go to McGill. All kinds of people told me that I should go to a Catholic college. The Sacred Heart nuns, however, did not pressure me. They were not the kind of people who would pressure you. In fact, one of the reasons I entered was that they never pushed me or told me I had a vocation and should enter. The alternative to McGill was the English department of Marguerite Bourgeois College. The English had a wing there and when I was about to begin college the girls were still wearing uniforms. I couldn't balance going to university with wearing uniforms. To me that wasn't university so I said that I wasn't going there. I asked my father about going to McGill and he said he would always find the money for whatever education I wanted. The attitude and atmosphere in the family was that you had to be improving yourself and learning. Also McGill was just at the top of our street because we were still living downtown then. When people told me that I would lose my faith at McGill it never for a moment occurred to me that I would. I was so sure of my faith, though I have to confess that when I was there I did have my doubts. The thing that saved me was reading G.K. Chesterton— I have the greatest love and respect for him. I read his *St. Francis of Assisi* and *Orthodoxy*, which was a discussion of the Church. At any rate, that settled me.

After McGill I went to the CND's business school, the Mother House. By Christmas time we were supposed to be practicing typing a couple of hours a day and Stephen Leacock, whose courses I had taken at McGill, advertised for someone to type a book for him. So I said I might as well practice on Leacock and type his book. I went to see him and he never asked me a single question. He just said I should meet him at his house at such a time. He lived on Côte-des-Neiges across the street from the convent. I typed a book for him on the British

Commonwealth and I had to do a little research such as phoning to get statistics on how many immigrants there were in certain years. He put a typewriter in the living room downstairs. When I went to his office I could see why. He had piles of papers that went literally to the ceiling on one side of his desk and the other side was almost as bad. I used to think that he would knock the whole pile down if he ever wanted to take one paper out. It was interesting work and it was fun. Sometimes I would go and work for half an hour or two hours and other times there would be no work at all. So I made money by practicing on Leacock. I had to do six copies because he was sending the book to five publishers and, of course, he kept one copy for himself. I liked him. First, because he never bothered me and because he was fascinating. I loved his classes although he wasn't humorous when he taught. He opened the door with his hand through an opening in the gown that professors wore in those days, and from the minute he opened the door he started teaching. He was a very learned man and I still remember the other students borrowing my notes because they couldn't follow him.

I worked for two years as a secretary in an engineers' office. I never found it interesting being a secretary and I never was a perfect typist even with practice. I also had a serious boyfriend and nearly married. When I realized I had a vocation I considered the Carmelites. I wrote to them in Three Rivers because I didn't want to enter a convent in my home town. They told me I would have to enter in Montreal so that was the end of my Carmelite vocation. Then I entered the Sacred Heart Novitiate in Albany, New York and I was there for two years. I didn't enter the order to teach, in fact I had no desire to teach, but once I began I just loved it and was very good at it. I taught and then became headmistress for about twenty years. I was headmistress at the two schools in Montreal, in Halifax and at Eden Hall in Philadelphia. Then I was Superior in Vancouver and then at the City House and I left when I was sixty-five years old. I also taught when I was the Superior but the Order doesn't want you in a classroom when you're sixty-five and mostly you don't want to go into a classroom either.(laughs)

In my fourth-high religion classes I used the social teachings of the Church and did a good deal of reading on the subject. I had a great desire to do something along the lines of what my episcopal brother Billy had done working for many years with the Young Christian Workers. When I was cloistered I couldn't go out to do anything in the way of helping the poor. After Vatican Council II when cloister was lifted and I learned about the *avocats populaires* who were helping welfare people, I became interested. I talked to Father Guy Bouillet who was the pastor of St. Cunegonde. He had been our chaplain for five years and I'll be grateful to him until I die for encouraging me to get involved in working in Little Burgundy. Sister Annette Archambault was an austere woman who thought that we were getting *embourgeoisées* so I asked her if she would be willing to come and live in Little Burgundy with me. She accepted and then Sister Alice Amyot joined us so we were three. I took a course with the *avocats populaires* on Bill 26. It was the law which came out in 1969 that gave welfare people the right to a subsistence. They asked me to work with them and so things came together. I also read a good deal about Liberation Theology and felt that, though God is everywhere, He is particularly where the poor are, and I wanted to be where God was. I'd spent many years of my life working with the rich and the super rich. I used to encourage giving to charity and many of our students and their parents gave money to help the poor but I never said that we have to change the world and not have all these poor people. What I teach now is that we've got to change the world so these people don't need our handouts. What bothers me is not individual selfishness but the structures that are in place which exploit people. Pay low wages—fire as soon as you're losing a little profit—fire all kinds of people who then have no employment.

There were many people who opposed my plans. Many felt that I should have stayed and helped the Sacred Heart School but you know, I'm not Irish for nothing, I've had the luck of the Irish all the way. I was the elected delegate from Canada to the General Chapter in Rome in 1970. The Major Superiors go but there's an elected delegate from every province. We are present in seven Latin American countries including Mexico, Puerto Rico and Cuba. These sisters were already involved with the Medellin Document. The bishops of Latin America met in 1968 in Medellin in Colombia and they realized that they were aligned with the rich and they had to change and align themselves more with the poor. This became know as Liberation Theology. Gustavo Gutierrez from Peru was a great support to me. "There's no way that I can tell the Sacred Heart nuns that they should be going to the poor," I said. He said, "You have to begin. You have to begin." At the Chapter in 1970 we took "options" and one of the options was greater solidarity with the poor, the second was greater solidarity with the Third World and the third was to maintain our mission of education even in our private schools. We've been so lucky because we've had Superiors who were listeners. Concha Comacho who was the Mother General at that time, saw clearly that we had to go more to the poor. We had free schools from 1800 when we were founded which was extremely prophetic because then no one was teaching the poor. St. Madeleine Sophie, our founder, established free schools which were attached to every boarding school or private school. In the process of history, public schools were established everywhere and by 1970 we confronted the fact that we were founded to work with the poor but we had largely abandoned this work.

The movement I'm in is called ODAS (Organisation d'aide aux Assistés Sociaux). Our aim is to help welfare people run their own lives. We teach welfare recipients the law and what their rights are. We used to go to the welfare office with them because they were often too scared but now it's a rare case when we have to go. We don't do any formal education in the sense of training them for jobs or anything like that. That's somebody else's work. What we try to do is make them realize that they have a right to a job, a right to respect, a right to be heard and listened to like anybody else. They are "inferiorized" by all kinds of experiences. One of the worst examples was a woman on welfare who went with her cheque to a caisse populaire and the teller said to her neighbouring teller, "*C'est un autre parasite de la société.*" I asked this woman if she reported them to the manager? "Oh, non. J'avais trop besoin de mon argent."They're so frightened. People on welfare don't live; they survive. We have meetings every Thursday and we average about eighty people. We organize workshops where they learn to express themselves. We are also fighting Bill 37 which is the reform of welfare law. There are more than thirty groups with us now fighting this Bill. We are partially funded by Centraide and we get some money from religious communities and foundations like the Alexandre de Sève.

I'm a nun because I was seeking God in an absolute kind of way and I think that in my life I've always tried to follow where I thought I would find God. I've been here now since 1973 and I have not changed my ideas. Being here is not as consoling as being able to go to a nice, quiet chapel with flowers which is more conducive to prayer than demonstrating on a street saying, "*La taxe d'eau, on la paye pas.*" It's not a contemplative life but since it's in solidarity with the exploited and the poor, it's of God. Alice and I were talking about how we have to learn to find God in daily life—to be able to find Him in cooking a meal, in being tired shopping, in having a cold, you know, the nitty gritty of life. You have to have the faith, the contemplative capacity to find God there and not only in church and in the sacraments. I want to be doing something that will help to liberate people on whatever level I can.

James and Lola More

The Irish love to sing but very few can make it their career as did Jimmy More. He was a singer and master of ceremonies in Montreal when vaudeville was in its heyday. Being a professional entertainer meant that Jimmy was much in demand for the numerous concerts which were given in various church halls in Montreal and he was never able to say no when asked by a parish priest to help out. Born in 1908, Jimmy began singing when he was only eight years old at concerts given at Belmont School. During World War II, he went overseas as part of the Army Show which was put together to entertain the troops. During that time, he worked with Johnny Wayne and Frank Shuster who later became fixtures on the Canadian entertainment scene. Jimmy married Lola Valiquette, a dancer whose professional name was Lola Milroy. Lola and Jimmy worked together for many years. During this interview, Lola had many interesting things to contribute about their working life together. Her comments are also included as they describe so well what it was like to be a vaudevillian in Montreal when entertainers like Charles Laughton and Agnes Moorehouse would come to town.

The name More is Scottish. I looked it up when I was in the army. It comes from Muir. My grandfather on my father's side was a true Scotsman who spoke with a heavy burr. My dad was born in Griffintown and he used to say that he was Canadian, period. He never mentioned that he was of Scottish descent. Primarily, my culture as I was growing up was Irish because my mother's name was Elizabeth Donnelly and I used to attend all the Irish parades and concerts.

My mother's brother, Joe Donnelly, was a sportsman and a singer, a baritone. When he and my mother were growing up in Griffintown, he used to come in at two o'clock in the morning and wake my poor, dear mother up. She was able to play the piano and he'd say, "Lizzie, I've got a new song," and he'd rehearse the song at that hour of the morning. Joe Donnelly was one of the first hockey players who left Canada to play in the United States. He settled in Pittsburgh with his wife and family and became quite a goaler. There are pictures of him up at the Montreal Amateur Athletic Association. He also worked all the sporting events in Pittsburgh. He was an announcer and he could stand in the middle of a ball park and without a microphone or any assistance he'd say, "LADIES AND GENTLEMEN, PITCHING FOR THE FIFTH TODAY ..." They could hear him all over the place.

I was born in St. Anthony's Parish and the first time I left St. Anthony's was when I got married. It was called the West End in those days and the English and the French got along beautifully. I spent two years at Belmont School on Guy Street. It was all lay teachers and one of the teachers, Mr. Cuddihy, was the director of music. My singing career really began when I was about eight years old and was in Mr. Cuddihy's Variety Club. He was a great man and I have good memories of him. After Belmont School, I attended St. Patrick's School which was on the corner of La Gauchetière and St. Genevieve. We had the Christian Brothers who were strict but we thank them today for that. Brother Walter was the director and you wouldn't fool around with him. He'd be there Monday to Friday checking you out as you came in every morning. His arms would be folded and he had a very innocent look on his face and you'd say, "Good morning, Brother." He'd say "Good morning, Jim," and if you were five minutes late or something, he'd wait until you passed him and then WHAM with a hand like a ham. He was great, though. Once a year we'd play hockey against the brothers and you had to be prepared to play rough and knock the daylights out of them or else they'd really do a job on you.

I got most of my training from the St. Patrick's Chancel Choir. We used to dress in suits with Eton collars and there were probably forty to forty-five members of the choir singing at all the Masses. In those days it wasn't easy because we had to do a Mass on Sunday morning and Vespers on Sunday night so we didn't have much time to fool around. Brother Joseph was the choirmaster but we had to answer to Brother Walter, too. If you came to school on Monday morning and you hadn't been at the services, you had to have a good excuse ready for Brother Walter because he'd lift you off your feet if you didn't.

When I was in my late teens, I belonged to the Unity Club of St. Patrick's. We used Congress Hall as our meeting place. The teenagers used to get together there rather than going out on the street which they do today. Father McShane and Father Doran used to come and mingle with the boys, especially on Sunday nights. Father Doran played the clarinet. Some of the fellows that I remember from the Unity Club are Billy Doyle and Eddy Cooney. Billy Doyle (Lord have mercy on his soul) was my neighbour in St. Anthony's and he became the organist and choirmaster at St. Patrick's Church. If we put on a musical play, Billy would get the volunteers for the all-male show. The girls would have a show of their own which might be a three-act play. Eddy Cooney was usually our leading man in the plays that we put on. In later years, the Unity Club also had a hockey team and we used to play out at Loyola.

I wish I had a penny for every time I visited St. Ann's Hall. They had about four concerts a year including St. Patrick's Day so there'd be three other plays that I was called upon to sing in. When the telephone first came out there were about fourteen Irish Catholic parishes. I kid around today and I say, "I did all of them." The fourteen parish priests, they all knew me. They used to phone me and I'd say to my dear mother, "That's the phone again. It's another one of the priests calling. They want my services again. I've given them my services last year and the year before that." My mother would say, "Be glad that you have a voice to do it. The Lord gave it to you." The argument was over then. I had to go.

I used to sing a lot at the Catholic Sailors' Club. I'd work solo in concerts organized by various parishes and Catholic clubs. They had the Montreal Sailors' Club, too, which was non-Catholic and I went there too. It was nice to go down there, see the sailors and wonder about their lives: what they did, why they were there and who looked after them. They were certainly well taken care of while they were on shore here. Lola and I would also play in armouries and hospitals. There were so many of these shows and I never regretted doing these benefits because of the great effect they had on the people who were there. When you are the MC you have to do the whole show and you can't leave until the end. A single act could come in and go out when they were finished. Many times I worked when I was sick and should have stayed in bed. It was a normal thing to do. You just did it and didn't complain.

I worked at all the places when I was in vaudeville: Krausman's Lorraine Grill, the Corona Hotel on Guy Street, the Princess and all the other theatres. The Princess was number one. You didn't get in there unless you were practically a star. They had an eight-act change of bill every week and that came directly from the Palace Theatre in New York City. In New York, if you made the Palace Theatre, you were in. The same applied to the Princess, it was Class A Vaudeville, two shows a day. Some of the other vaudeville theatres were doing four or five shows a day. I remember going to the Princess as a kid. I'd go up the escalator to the "gods" and for two cents you got a program to follow the acts. You could also buy an ice-cream bar or something, too. The big time had such an effect on me. It was really big time. When you consider that a performer would get out on the stage of the Princess, no microphone, no assistance, just his voice and his God-given talent. You revelled in that and today, I still do. When I hear them all fussing over a mike today, I just shake my head and say, "My gosh."

I worked with Jack Benny and Kate Smith. They were nice people but you didn't have much time to get close to them to talk. My favourite was Mahalia Jackson. I saw her in the dressing room of the Place des Arts when she did a show there. Our agency booked her and when she came out on stage they didn't fuss with a mike for her. She knew exactly what she wanted. I wasn't too crazy about folk songs or gospel singing but she converted me. What a singer and what a performer! The French-Canadian people used to pack the hall to hear her.

The Princess was up on St. Catherine Street near St. Alexander Street and Congress Hall was down on Dorchester. Monsignor McShane was a great businessman. He would say, "Oh, look who's in at the Princess this week. It just fits in with our little show that we're doing." So somebody would have to go with Father McShane and talk one of the acts into coming down to St. Patrick's.

Do you know who we brought in there? The Virginia Judge, he was called. He was second to close,(that's what we called a top act). His name was Walter Kelly and he was Grace Kelly's uncle. He used to do a one-man act.

I remember when our agency booked Mickey Rooney. We all went down to the train to meet him, including the club owner and the booking agent of Paramount Entertainment. Later, we were in the Mount Royal Hotel where he was staying. He walked across the lobby of the hotel as though he owned the place. He was followed by a blonde (I don't know which wife it was. He had about eight.) He went up to the mezzanine floor to have a press conference and everybody was following Mickey. I'll never forget that day.

(Lola More: Organizations like the Masons and the Knights of Columbus used to have shows so we'd get a call directly from them. On New Year's Eve, we used to do eight or nine shows starting at midnight. It was the biggest night of the year. We'd work all the big theatres, the Princess, (that was the best) the Palace, the Capitol, Loew's, the Orpheum, all the big theatres. I'd stay in the same costume and it was very interesting how it worked: you'd be first on at the Palace, then you'd put slacks and a coat over your costume and a driver would take you to the next theatre where you'd be the third act. At the next theatre you'd be the fifth act and you'd do the whole circuit like that. You'd finish at around four or five in the morning at the Engineer's Club or the St. George's Club. During the Depression, people were looking for entertainment. Our salaries weren't big but this town was wide open in the thirties and you could work without stop for weeks. You might even be in one place for a year or two. I usually stayed two weeks in one place. I could work for six months in Montreal and then go down to the States. There was so much work available. When Jimmy worked at clubs like the Savoy and the Montmartre, he usually stayed for eighteen months. We had a booking agent who arranged things for us. The Bellevue Casino was a very nice place too. They had a line of girls but today there's nothing. Things started to change in the fifties. When I was working, the girls could walk on St. Catherine Street at four o'clock in the morning after a late show and nobody would bother them. When our son David was born I could still work because he was a good traveller and he came everywhere with us. When our daughter Marilyn was born I stopped working because it was a little difficult with the two of them.)

I went overseas twice in World War II because I was active in the Canadian Army Show. I was in Scotland, Holland and Italy. I was in the army for about four years and it was a good experience. The Canadian Army Show was mostly built up in Toronto and most of the people were Torontonians. It was a good show because we had the pick of all the musicians in Canada, anyone we wanted. The army would see a good saxophone player and say, "You're in." Our group had four or five members of the Toronto Symphony. When the war was over, many of these musicians went back to work as professionals.

The Navy Show could only play halls and auditoriums whereas the Army Show played right in the front lines. When we got overseas we were broken up into five units instead of one big unit because the big units couldn't play the front lines very well, could they? So the talent was split up and the different units would follow the troops and play different camps in various places. I was fortunate, I got into a group that had thirteen of the original musicians of the big show. Wayne and Shuster were in our group and we also had a girl from Hollywood, Ida Broadbent, as our choreographer. We had to build our own stages and everything. On one occasion, the sergeant major told us that the piano would have to be down in a ravine but, "Be very careful because we've just mined the whole place." We let somebody else lift the piano and we got out of there fast. There were some close calls for me in London, too. I got to know a pub in London and anytime I went in and there was an air raid, they would say, "Get him to sing, I don't want to lose the customers." I had to sing while they were bombing.

I'm happy that I could make entertaining people my life's work. I was always happy to do shows. Maybe I complained sometimes about doing benefit shows because I figured that if someone did typing in an office five days a week and somebody asked them to go out and type, would they get paid or would they do it for nothing? What do I like best about being an entertainer? The applause and the bows. Lola and I still like it, believe me. I worked the fortieth anniversary party for Our Lady of Fatima Parish and the hall was packed to the roof.

If I were to give advice to a young man today about choosing a career, I'd tell him to choose sports of any kind. If he could master golf, he'd be in line for a profitable existence. Montreal was never a good town for the top singers or vaudevillians. The thought used to run through my mind when I was young that I should go to the States but I never took it seriously. I was the only one at home and it made it tough to leave. Sentimentality was also a factor so I made a lot less money and stayed here.

Do I have any regrets in life? My only regret is that I didn't find a girl like Lola sooner than I did. We got engaged when I was working as a cruise director on the Saguenay for the Canada Steamship Lines on the *Richelieu*. We went to Ste. Anne de Beaupré and I gave her the ring there. We had the ring blessed there, too.

Lola (second from left) and Jimmy with two other dancers dressed
for a Gay 90s review. The show was performed at the Savoy Café
on St. Alexander Street, one of the many clubs providing
entertainment during the 1930s and 1940s.
Photo by Gaby of Montreal. Courtesy of Marilyn Sudia.

Francis (Frank) Hanley

No one is more identified with Griffintown than Frank "Banjo" Hanley. His long and colourful career includes stints as a jockey, prize fighter, soft shoe dancer, politician and the area's favourite elf in the annual St. Patrick's Parade. He was twice ejected by police from Montreal City Hall meetings, once for opposing Jean Drapeau's plan to legalize the sale of horsemeat in 1969. "Horses are for riding, not eating " was his position. During the Depression while working for a coal company he saw his chance to become a modern-day Robin Hood. He and his fellow workers would fill 100-pound bags with eighty pounds of coal. Westmount residents would pay the full amount for their shrunken bags while the missing twenty pounds of coal found their way into the frigid homes of Griffintown's needy. St. Ann's elections were sometimes rigged but Frank Hanley always maintained that his boys just liked baseball and that was why they brought their bats to work with them at campaign headquarters. In spite of his sometimes unorthodox methods, Frank has many supporters who remember his generosity, thoughtfulness and help when they. needed it most.

I was born in 1909 in Griffintown. All my mother's people, the Johnsons, were originally Protestant but they all turned Catholic. My father's family were all Catholics. When I was very young, she and my father (who was on crutches), took me up to St. Joseph's Oratory. She went up the steps praying on her knees and my father left his crutches up at the Oratory.

Griffintown, including Victoriatown, was full of neighbourly people. If someone was ill, the next door neighbour would take care of him. Let's say it was one of the best areas in the city at the time, as far as the neighbours were concerned, and there was no question of crime then, either. The No. 7 Police Station was on Young Street and Jimmy Williams was in charge of the Black Maria which was pulled by two horses. My grandfather was the stable man for Jimmy Feron's, the undertaker, and the police captain and some of his men would come to the stable for card games and a drink while I took care of the station next door. I was five. When I was older, I used to go with Jimmy Williams to pick up those who were drunk and couldn't make it home. We'd take them in to be sobered up and send them home. They were strong men and they could drink. There were no problems with beating up the kids or the wife. It was a different kind of society.

Was St. Ann's School tough? You better believe it! We had to wear a shirt and tie, short pants and golf stockings, as they called them. Many of the children couldn't afford to dress fancy but they did the best they could. You had to be ready with your homework done and there was no talking back to the teachers. They were tough. On the first Friday of the month we lined up in school and were marched to the church. You'd better be in church for Communion every Sunday too. I think that's what's missing in the school program today. I think we would have a better society if we were living today as we lived then.

If you graduated from St. Ann's School, the doors of the CNR and other companies were wide open. You started in the twelfth class and finished in the first class. In first class they had higher education so when you were finished you were really qualified. That's why the CPR and other companies were packed with former St. Ann's pupils. You walked right in. Eddy Shanahan became secretary to Sir Montagu Allan.

I was asked to leave St. Ann's when I was twelve years old because I rode a pony in the St. Patrick's Parade, as my father insisted, instead of walking with my class. My father had an argument with the principal. They were two stubborn Irishmen, the principal and my father. The principal said, "He's gonna walk." My father said, "He's gonna ride." "He's gonna walk." "He's gonna ride." So I rode myself right out of school, but I don't think I did so badly without an education. I got my first job at Lyman's Limited on St. Paul Street. My next job was checking cheese coming in from England at the docks. Then I went to work for Crane for a while and it was when I was working there that I started a boxing career. I was fortunate to win both the city and provincial boxing championships. I weighted 108 pounds and was a flyweight.

I liked horses so I decided to go on tour as a jockey. I started training here at Delormier Park and then I was signed up by George Bridge of Florida and I went away with him. I was with him for about five years. I had a great career at all the race tracks in America and one in Havana. Then it got too tough. I couldn't make the weight anymore and I sprained an ankle. To keep your weight down you had to put on winter underwear when it was 110 degrees and run around the track. Some of the horses were very tough to handle and I had to learn by myself....how to hold the head up in the air so it wouldn't get away and so on and so forth. I was very, very attached to horses and I cared too much about them to take any kind of chances.

As I grew older we hit the Depression. I was married then and we had to go and work for our welfare. People on welfare had to work regardless if you were a cripple and I appreciate that today—that we had to work. We worked on Taschereau Boulevard, the Boardwalk, and at the Botanical Gardens. It wasn't easy during the winter months on Taschereau Boulevard. There was one Frenchman who had only one leg. The other one had been crushed and he had to work carrying water to the men working on the roads in the summer.

During this time, there was a chap by the name of Couturier and he said, "Frank, we got to do something about this forcing people to work on Taschereau Boulevard in the damp and cold without food. Let's form an association." We wanted to improve conditions for the men, like not working if it was too cold. We had an office on Charlevoix Street which was rent-free and we organized and prepared for the next (municipal) election. When 1940 came along, I was opposed by St. James Street and the Businessmen's Association but I won that election easily. That tempted me to run for the National Assembly of Quebec in 1948. I won that and stayed until I retired in 1970.

In politics I was the only one to hit the top out of St. Ann's—from councillor for thirty years at city hall, four years as vice-president of the City Executive Committee, acting mayor of the City of Montreal and twenty-two years in the National Assembly. I ran as an independent all the time. I was very friendly with Duplessis. I was friendly with them all. Did I ever hear of dead people voting? Oh, I think I'd have to be paid for such secrets! Actually, I'd be the first to do it and I'd have fun. They all telegraphed. You'd go up to the cemetery and look at the tombstones and get a list of names. At that time, the returning officer would have a meeting with the chief returning officer and they'd take the ballot boxes home. They'd pack the boxes at night at home...the box was half-filled before the election started. I can't give you more than that. I didn't say I would do that. Let's just say that most of them would.

In the summertime I used to have movies and street dances and I got the biggest bands and biggest entertainers from Hollywood whenever they were in town playing at the El Morocco or the Bellevue Casino. That was to keep the people busy. They had no summer homes, no place to go; they just sat on the curb. I met Bob Hope, Bing Crosby....name them, I met them all. And Jimmy Durante too. When he was here I invited him to present a trophy to the winners of the first boys' curling championship, a French group from the Point. I had a Murray Hill bus go to the Mount Royal Hotel where Jimmy was staying. We had a big Italian brass band and all the cars were lined up. When Jimmy came out he saw a sign that said: BANK ON FRANK, VOTE FOR HANLEY. He said, "Geez, Frank, I didn't know it was an election parade. Now let's go to work." And then it was in and out of every tavern from the Mount Royal to Marguerite Bourgeoys Park, and he enjoyed it. I said, "Okay Jimmy, now it's the presentation and you've got to make a French speech." "Geez, Frank, I can't even speak English." He later took some of my friends up to a restaurant for roast beef and paid the bill.

When Sarto Fournier was entertaining the Queen at the Queen Elizabeth Hotel, I decided to put on the Queen's Ball of the Masses at Marguerite Bourgeoys Park. I got 10,000 pages people that night. I asked one of the singers from the Bellevue Casino if he wanted to sing at the Queen's Ball of the Masses. "Oh, yes," he said, so I sent two detectives up in a car to pick him up. They swung by the Queen Elizabeth Hotel and asked, "Isn't this where the Ball is?" They never answered—kept driving him down to the park. It was jammed. He said, "I've been fooled." We told him that this was the Ball for the Masses and not to worry, we had a band to play his music. No problem at all. He was a tremendous success. I got all the publicity the following day because the guests at the Queen's reception rushed her and stood on the tables, and I had 10,000 well-controlled people at the park.

Once the garbage men went on strike. The city was bankrupt and they wanted the men to go out at night and help the Roads Department clear the streets after a snowstorm. They were all my gang because Couturier was in the Incineration Department and he started me off in politics. The city manager called me up and said, "Frank, we've got to settle this strike of your gang." "Okay," I says, "I'll talk to them." They called a meeting and the garbage men said, "Look, we have to do something for Frank. How about helping to clean up the city?" Some asked what they were going to get out of it. That was tough work they did, lifting the barrels, and what they'd do when they'd go to the dump was drop into the grocery store and have a couple of quarts of beer while the driver was busy, and he'd pick them up on the way back. "Tell you what I'll do," I said. "I'll make it legal." Parent agreed. A bottle or two of beer was nothing. I settled that strike for a bottle of beer.

I got everything I wanted from Duplessis. I had no problem with him. He always gave me a grant for the St. Patrick's Day Parade. He loved the Irish. He was a darn good Catholic, too. He was at St. Patrick's Church every Sunday and every Wednesday he'd be at the Cathedral in Quebec. He helped everyone. The English couldn't understand him. He was good to them and he died broke. He liked fun, too. For instance, his bodyguard had the patronage of running the cock show in St. Saveur on the weekends. Duplessis said, "Frank, I'm going to play a trick on him." He sent the Provincial Police in and they raided his bodyguard's cock fight. He had the police take all the chickens and put them in cells. One time Drapeau wrote a letter to all my constituents telling them that the Pope didn't want me to get elected. I wish I still had that letter. Anyway, Duplessis said that Drapeau was butting in and gave me so much money for that election that I swept Drapeau under. I beat him and the Pope on the same day.*

*In the provincial election of 1956, Duplessis bought the election for Hanley as a way to annoy Jean Drapeau. The two men clashed on many issues and Drapeau was to feel Duplessis's wrath again when the Union Nationale electoral machine managed to get Sarto Fournier elected as mayor in 1957.

Frank Hanley, the first ever Irishman of the Year, enjoying a drink
with Mayor Pierre Bourque at a St. Patrick's Party,
Montreal City Hall, 1997.
Photo by Denis Labine, Ville de Montréal.
Courtesy of Frank Hanley.

Patrick James (Percy) Taugher

Percy Taugher was born on May 6, 1909 in Griffintown but the family later moved to Coursol Street in the West End. The Taughers were a well-known family in Griffintown. They were very active in sports, politics and community organizations. Percy Taugher's great-uncle John Taugher owned a store on the corner of Smith (later changed to Wellington) and McCord (Mountain) which was a popular gathering spot in the neighbourhood.

When I was born the family was living at 163 McCord Street in Griffintown. We later moved to 149 McCord in what was known as Griffin's Block. The Griffins were comfortably off and they owned many properties on McCord and Eleanor Streets. Mary Ann was an old maid. Her brother Mike, who was married and had a family, worked as a rod man for the City of Montreal. I think there were other Griffins living uptown on Mountain Street.

My father was William John and my mother was Margaret Ann Shields. They were born in Canada of Irish descent. Grandpa Shields worked for the Montreal Light, Heat and Power and he and my grandmother had four children. My mother had two brothers; Johnny, who died when he was only twenty-one, and Jimmy, who never married. She and her sister Lizzie both married.

Dad was known as W. J. Tucker at work and when he died in 1939 I straightened out the spelling of the family name. I wrote a letter to the secretary of the company and accused him of having made a mistake so it was changed to Taugher. The story is that Grandma Taugher, whose first name was Hannah, was eight or ten years younger than Grandpa and when he'd come home from work in the afternoon she'd be skipping out on the sidewalk. She must have been sixteen or seventeen at the time. She used to joke, "Hannah asked him and Paddy took her (Tucker)." There used to be a stained-glass window in St. Ann's Church with THE TAUGHER FAMILY written on it. I'm sorry I didn't try to get it when the church was torn down.

Grandpa Taugher played lacrosse for the Shamrocks and so did his brother Johnny whom we always called Uncle Johnny. James McShane* was the mayor of Montreal then and we have a picture of Grandpa with the lacrosse stick and Mayor McShane pointing to him. My wife's father also played for the Shamrocks. They all wore the special padded hats with a peak in the front and back and they used to play at their grounds in Mile End.

Uncle Johnny owned a store right across from St. Ann's Church. He was a tall, bald man from what I can remember. He had three or four daughters and two sons, Danny and Jackie. Danny studied for the priesthood for seven years. In those days, the Redemptorists paid for the first seven years of your education and then the family had to pay for the rest. He came home one Easter morning after the seventh year and announced that he wasn't going back. Danny never married but one of his sisters married a McDonnell who later ran the store and it became known as The Coffee Pot. When Uncle Johnny ran the store, it was a restaurant and they also sold sweets. Every night, Uncle Johnny would take the unsold sweets and give them away to people. Grandpa Taugher was a Liberal, through and through, but Uncle Johnny was a Conservative because Alderman O'Connell was a Conservative. Uncle Johnny was a wardheeler (a local worker for a political boss) in St. Ann's. He was O'Connell's right hand man. If some old widow wanted two bags of coal, O'Connell referred her to Uncle Johnny. He was also a justice of the peace and had authority to sign documents.

I was the oldest of five children and then came my sister, Everilda (ritzy name in those days) who died young. Then there was John and the twins, Eunice and Phyllis. Mama was tall and thin and Dad was a big man, not too tall but he wore a size-eighteen collar and was a great sportsman. He was an assistant supervisor of the Montreal Light, Heat and Power shops at the corner of Ann and Ottawa. I remember very clearly my brother John's baptism at St. Ann's. He was born on St. Joseph's Day, the 19th of March. Dad always did things well and he had a coach come to the house at 149 McCord. The driver sat outside and the godmother, godfather and Dad sat inside the coach with my baby brother. I remember hanging on to the big springs at the back of the coach and going down McCord to the Baptism. I also remember going to Currie's, a tailor shop on Notre Dame Street, to get my made-to-order First Communion suit. When I got my first pair of ice skates, I would skate down McCord Street on the streetcar tracks with a broomstick to the rink at Gallery Square.

I started school at St. Ann's and the classes went backwards. Eleven was the baby class and you went 10-9-8-7-6 finishing with 1. I started in grade ten with Brother Macedonia who had also taught my father. He had a scheme worked out in his mind. When my father gave me too much help with my homework, Brother Macedonia would give him eight and give me two. Sometimes it would be reversed when I did my own homework. Brother James, the principal, was a big man and he was nuts on mental arithmetic. Each classroom had an entrance door but there was also a connecting door between the classes. He would open the door, walk in and he'd start 22,44,67. By the time he reached the other door we were expected to have the correct total. He was a bug on that. Brother

Hubert would let us take off our shoes and warm our feet on the radiator when it was cold in wintertime. I went to that school for three or four years and then the family moved to Coursol Street. I tried Belmont School on Guy Street. It was a lay school and my father didn't like it too much so he sent me to St. Gabriel's School in Point St. Charles.

As a young lad in Griffintown I used to spend my Sundays over at the No. 3 Fire Station on Young and Ottawa. I would go to watch my dad and Uncle John play pool. There was always an altar set up at the fire station for the Corpus Christi procession and my dad used to supply the lighting for this altar. "Bull" Fennell** was the captain at the police station on Young Street between Ottawa and Wellington. He was a bluff man. I remember once one of his officers had to destroy a cat that they had put in a barrel. He looked the other way and unloaded his pistol. Boom! Boom! It took about six shots before he killed the cat.

On Saturday mornings I used to go shopping with Grandma Shields. We'd come out the back door on McCord Street, go up Eleanor and then along Little Eleanor to Notre Dame and then go along to Masterman's Butcher Shop. It was a packing company near Colborne Street. There was a gateway you'd enter with steps and then there was a long loading dock. We would go to a little man with a black moustache and Grandma would order her steaks. He would take them out from under the counter and stick his index finger in them to show that they were tender. Then she would give him the rest of her order and she always gave him a quarter tip, in those days it was quite a tip. There were many other stores in the neighbourhood where she used to shop like Harry Laniel's Grocery Store on the corner of Barré and McCord, McArans General Store which was run by an Irish couple and Pegnem's Fish Market.

When Grandma Shields died, I was only six years old. She died in 1917 at the age of seventy-two. There were two priests in the room, Father Flood from St. Anthony's and a young curate, Father O'Rourke from St. Raphael's. She was laid out at home. They served sandwiches and other things and there were clay pipes and a big bowl of shag tobacco. Heaven forbid if you ever dozed off. They got the black shoe polish and painted your face. The Malones and the McCarthys were there and some of the people, mostly the men, stayed all night. When we were kids, one of the things we would do as we walked down the street was to count the holes on the top of the door where the crepes had been hung. That was one of our pastimes. If there were four holes, that meant that there had been four funerals there over the years.

The house at number 91 Coursol where we moved had belonged to the vice-president of Imperial Tobacco. It was quite a house. The number was later changed to 2391. It had a stone front and next door to us was a tea merchant, Mr. Brown. We had a shed in the back and a big hot-water furnace in the corner of the downstairs kitchen. There was also a pantry, a small bathroom and a downstairs dining room. The middle floor had the upstairs dining room, the parlour with a fireplace and Dad's den. The parlour and dining room were really one big room with pillars dividing it. Upstairs on the third floor was the family bathroom and three bedrooms. My dad used to go to my Aunt Gallagher's in Griffintown for lunch and pay her so much a week instead of going all the way home for lunch.

My brother, John, was always crazy mad about ponies and Grandpa Taugher, who lived across the street on Coursol, helped my father build a box stall in the woodshed in the lane at the back. My dad bought him a pony and the stablemaster of Montreal Light, Heat and Power, John Hughes, kept it at their stable at the corner of Young and Ottawa. My Uncle Frank and I went down Christmas Eve and brought this pony home to Coursol Street. We walked along Ottawa Street and up Seigneurs holding the long reins as it hadn't been broken for harness yet. We put it in the stall and Christmas morning when my brother came down he saw the bridle hanging on the fireplace, Dad said, "Well, you'd better go out and see." He went out and came back, "A pony! A real live pony!" That altered how we celebrated St. Patrick's Day because my brother could then ride in the parade although I had to walk with him to control the pony because of all the bands and the excitement. We had a cutter in the wintertime with "Tucker Brothers", not "Taugher", written on the side of it and during Christmas holidays we used to go up Atwater to the mountain with the pony and the cutter. We'd come home at lunchtime and tie "Betty" to a tree outside the door. Then we'd go in through the bottom door, have lunch, and come out and go up again. Betty was always twice as fast coming home and would race hell-bent for election down Atwater Avenue.

We used to have an Airedale named Sport and Dad also got a little goat to put in the stall with the pony. The vet told him that a goat would pick up any sicknesses before the pony did. Father had built an alleyway between the shed and the house so that we didn't have to go outdoors to feed Betty in the morning. We'd open the door and out would come the goat, down the stairs and into the kitchen, tat, tat, tat, tat, walking all over the floor. Sport would attack the goat and the goat would butt Sport with her little horns so it was quite a menagerie.

I believe that my mother and father thought they were going to be childless because they were married four years before I came along so Aunt Lizzie's daughter, Lottie, came to live in my parent's home. She was about four or five years older than me. I wasn't really in her sphere but I remember that she used to engineer many parties at our house. Maybe eight or ten couples would be invited. They'd roll back the rugs for dancing and play the gramophone. We had a piano as well and I think it was a Howard. Then they would all go downstairs to eat. Lottie went with Gerald Furlong and her friend Barbara went with Gerry Hayes. They would all meet at the corner of Vinet and Coursol and walk down Vinet Street to Charlevoix and then walk home again together. My friends were mostly boys from the Victoria Rifles. One had a sax and my Uncle Jimmy, who was quite a song and dance man, played the piano by ear. In fact, one of the promoters here wanted to take him to New York but it never materialized.

After St. Gabriel's School, I went to Catholic High on Durocher Street. I finished high school on June 6, 1925 and went down for a job interview to the Montreal Light, Heat and Power. In those days there was no personnel department, each superintendent hired his own people. It was Friday afternoon and I was interviewed by a Mr. Turley. He hired me and told me that I would get a better job at the head office on Craig Street. I told him that I preferred to work in the shop so he said, "Well, fine, you can start Monday." I said, "What's the matter with this afternoon?" It was one o'clock on Friday afternoon and I couldn't wait to start work. I was sixteen years old when I began working and I left due to a heart condition in 1955 with thirty years' service.

The Depression didn't affect our family. In fact, I think we were better off. Dad had a steady job, I was working and prices were low. When World War II started, my brother John went overseas with the Royal Canadian Artillery. He joined in Quebec as an officer in training. He went overseas as a 2nd lieutenant and was then promoted to lieutenant and then captain. He was wounded twice; once during the Battle of Britain and once in Italy.

My brother had played hockey for the Montreal Royals and for the Quebec Aces. Those were the top amateur teams in those days but they were semi-pro. John went to England and played hockey for the Brighton Tigers in the European League. There were two French teams and they were stocked with French Canadians while Brighton was stocked with English Canadians. John came back to Canada after the hockey season finished in 1937, I believe. I remember that he came back just before the coronation of George VI. I played a bit of hockey and I played baseball with the North Branch "Y" at Atwater Park.

My wife and I have been very happy. We've never had an argument that I can remember. We've enjoyed travelling and the togetherness with Beverley and her husband Joe.

* There have been three mayors of Montreal who have also served as president of the St. Patrick's Society: William Workman, Hon. James McShane and Dr. James J. Guerin.

** One of my favourite stories about the time when "Bull" Fennell was the police chief has to do with his raids on the blind pigs in the area. It seems that women would call the chief and complain that their men were spending too much time in the various blind pigs in the neighbourhood. "Bull" would take note of their complaints and proceed to uphold the law. He would arrange his men in military formation in the middle of Young Street and then, barking out orders in a very loud voice, "Hut, one, two, left, right" the contingent of men in blue would march to the blind pig in question making one terrible racket as they went. One had to be completely deaf not to hear them coming and by the time they arrived, everything was calm and normal in the house with not a customer in sight.(PB)

John and Percy Taugher and "Betty."
"During Christmas holidays we used to go up Atwater to the mountian with the pony and cutter."
Courtesy of Beverley Rozek.

95

John H. Sullivan

John H. Sullivan is the great-great-grandson of Lieutenant John O'Sullivan and Mary Landers. Lieut. O'Sullivan served in Wolfe Tone's army of United Irishmen in the rebellion of 1798. Due to the amnesty proclaimed by Lord Cornwallis, he was able to make his way to St. John's, Newfoundland and then later to Quebec. He settled near Quebec City with his family. Apparently unscathed by his unfortunate experience in Ireland, Lieutenant O'Sullivan soon became involved in directing the transportation of military supplies from Quebec to Montreal in the War of 1812. His son, John Owen, doing what so many Irishmen have done, married a French-Canadian girl in 1826. She was Marie Plamondon, the daughter of a respected land surveyor. They celebrated their golden wedding anniversary on January 24, 1876 and the *Daily Telegraph* of January 29th reported the following:

> When the religious ceremony was over, the married couple returned to Mr. O'Sullivan's house, followed by the guests, whilst musicians gaily played "Vive la Canadienne" and "St. Patrick's Day." A lunch, composed of dainty dishes, artistically arranged, was served to the happy guests; the rest of the day was devoted to entertainment; there were old-fashioned and modern dances - minuets, cotillons and quadrilles.

John H. Sullivan, son of Colonel John Alexander Sullivan, Q.C. and Corinne Hensley Bourgoin was born in Montreal and married Madeline Sidely Graham at the Ascension of Our Lord Church in 1937. He has met many world figures during his years of involvement in politics, both at the municipal, provincial and federal level. He was also the acting mayor of Montreal for a short but interesting time.

My family has been in Canada for almost two hundred years. My ancestors fought in the uprising of 1798 in Ireland which was ruthlessly put down by the English Army under the command of Lord Cornwallis. The Irish Army's defeat was due in some measure because the French Army, who were supposed to join the Irish in battle, were unable to do so due to the fact that the French Fleet could not land on account of unfavourable winds. So, after their defeat, many of the officers fled Ireland for different parts of the world. My ancestors arrived first in Newfoundland and then went to Quebec City. Many of the Irish at that time intermarried with the French because they shared the same religion. The Plamondons were engineers and land surveyors and so that's how so many Sullivans became land surveyors. My grandfather was a civil engineer and a land surveyor although my father became a lawyer. Originally, the name of the family was O'Sullivan and I believe the "O" was dropped because the priest forgot to put it on when he wrote the name.

My grandfather moved from Quebec City to Beauharnois where he was appointed engineer for the City of Beauharnois. Later, he moved to Valleyfield where he continued working as a civil engineer and land surveyor. He was elected mayor of the City of Valleyfield on four occasions. Valleyfield at that time was mostly English-speaking. My father, John Alexander Sullivan, QC, moved to Montreal around 1906 to practice law for the City of Notre Dame de Grâce. He also was a member of Parliament for St. Ann's at one time and he became deputy postmaster general of Canada and also a colonel of the Postal Corps.

Actually, I'm of Irish, French and Scottish descent. I was educated in English; first at Notre Dame College which had English classes in those days. Then I went to Querbes Academy and later to Catholic High where I was taught by the Irish Presentation Brothers. When I was born, we lived in Notre Dame de Grâce. I speak French fluently. Growing up, my friends and I didn't consider ourselves Irish, French, English or Scottish. We just considered ourselves Canadian and we all lived together very happily. When we went to house parties I can't recall if we spoke French or English because it didn't make any difference to us.

There used to be a lot of debutante balls notwithstanding the Great Depression. When I was young we were usually invited by the parents who gave dances in those days, not unlike now with the presentation of the debutantes at the St. Andrew's Ball. We went and danced with all the pretty girls. Most of those balls were held in hotels like the Ritz-Carlton. The number of guests would depend on how much money the father had to spend. (laughs) The parents would chaperone and everybody was well behaved. When I started to date, I dated mostly English-speaking girls.

The Depression didn't affect my family but war did. I lost an uncle in each of the World Wars. I personally served with the Royal Canadian Mounted Police Reserve during the Second World War.

I was a member of the Montreal City Council at one time and was the acting mayor of the City for about four months. Once I had to get the police to throw Frank Hanley out of the Council Chambers because he wanted to speak all the time. The topic was the Maurice Richard Riot. I guess you could say that Frank was one of the "fighting Irish." (laughs) I became a member of the St. Patrick's Society when Leo McKenna, who was also on the City Council approached me and asked me to run as a candidate.

I used to be a member of the Union Nationale because I came from a Conservative family. I knew Duplessis—he was a go-getter. He was very gregarious and had tremendous power which he used to his advantage and to the advantage of the Party. If a county didn't elect a member of the Union

Nationale, the roads weren't built in that county. He got things done but after a while, when a man is in power too long he tends to become corrupt.

I think that John Diefenbaker was a great prime minister. He was the guest of honour in 1962 when I organized the St. Patrick's Ball. I always remember asking him one day, "Mr. Prime Minister, we should have a new flag for Canada." He said, "Never. I fought in the First World War with the British emblem and I want to keep it that way." I think the present flag is a good one but I would have liked some blue in there too.

Once I was invited by Prime Minister Pearson to have lunch on Sussex Drive in Ottawa when President Eamon de Valera of Ireland came to Canada for a visit. At the end of the luncheon the prime minister asked everybody to stand up for a toast to her Majesty the Queen and everybody stood up except de Valera. He wouldn't stand up until his son, who was present said, "Father, it's the Queen of Canada." Then he stood up.(laughs) De Valera was a very tall, austere man who put a distance between himself and people. Later on in the evening the Irish ambassador to Canada gave a reception for him and I attended with some members of St. Patrick's Society. We had our piper who preceded us. Mr. de Valera was half blind and could hardly see. I told him, "Mr. President, our piper here is in an Irish kilt." He thanked me for that and he smiled.

John H. Sullivan in Ottawa on Canada Day in 1992.
One of his ancestors served in Wolfe Tone's army of
United Irishmen in the Rebellion of 1798.
Courtesy of John Sullivan.

Margaret Murphy Neville

Margaret Neville was born in Newfoundland on September 1, 1911 and came to Montreal as a young girl. It is always open house at the Neville's house in Verdun and one is always impressed by the warmth and loyalty all the members of this family show to one other and to their many friends.

My mother died when I was very young. My father left home and travelled and then he remarried. My sister Kathleen and I lived with my grandmother and my Aunt Sarah. They looked after us until we joined my father and my stepmother in Montreal.

We had a wonderful childhood in Newfoundland. I remember in the summers going around and picking berries and playing in my bare feet most of the time. We used to catch the little trout in the brook and bring them up and put them in my grandmother's well. She didn't appreciate that and used to get real angry. Our school was just across the brook, not far from our house. All we had to do was go over a little bridge and down the road and we were there but in the winter we were snowed in. We had to go up on the roof and climb down and shovel the snow away from the door so we could get out.

In the wintertime my grandmother used to buy a barrel of molasses and we used to get bulk sugar and flour and, of course, we had a cow. We had our own milk and cream and we used to help my grandmother make butter. We had a root cellar to store cabbage, turnips, carrots and potatoes from the garden. We also had a horse, a goat and some pigs.

My grandmother had this little place we called The Flakes out near the water. She used to clean the fish and spread them out on the flakes which were like built-up racks. Then she'd throw salt on them and leave them there to dry till they got as hard as a board and then you could pick them up and stack them one on top of the other. We'd store the fish and my grandmother would make all kinds of dishes with it like fish stew and fish and brewis. That's why today I'm not crazy about it. I had enough of it when I was small. (laughs)

My great-aunt and uncle lived not far from us, just down the road. Other families, the Olivers and the Johnsons were within walking distance. To get to church in Northern Bay we had to walk three miles there and back unless we got a lift with somebody with a horse and buggy.

Being a child, it wasn't a hard life at the time but it was hard for older people. You didn't have welfare or anything like that. Two of my grandmother's sons died and the other children all left home and went to Boston. My Uncle Art,

Margaret Murphy Neville (right) with her sister Kathleen in
Newfoundland, 1919. They were soon to travel
to Montreal to meet their new "mudder."
"My sister couldn't understand how you could get eggs and
milk at the grocery store because she didn't see any cows
and chickens around!"
Courtesy of Margaret Neville.

who lived with us, joined the navy and went off too so there was just my grandmother, my aunt, my sister and I living there.

I was about eight years old and my sister was two years younger when we left Newfoundland. She wanted to bring the calf on the train with us. My grandmother and aunt were brokenhearted and the day we left my grandmother went up in the woods and stayed there crying because she had looked after us so long and we were like her own children. We took a train and then a ferry but I don't remember much about it because I was really sick. We were travelling with my Aunt Ellen and her friend. When the train came into Place Viger Station, my father and stepmother came to meet us and as we were walking on the sidewalk outside the station, my sister turned to my stepmother and she put her hands on her hips and said, "Are you me new mudder? If you tink you're going to boss me you're not because I'm not going to do what you tell me to do."

It was a different life here. My sister couldn't understand how you could get eggs and milk at the grocery store because she didn't see any cows and chickens around. We got laughed at in school at first because it was, "dese, dose, dem" and naturally they didn't speak like that here.

We went to school at St. Dominic's. One of my teachers had those clappers that they used and when I didn't know the answer to a question she said I wasn't paying attention and she hit me on the knuckles with them. I started to cry and she kept me in during the lunch hour. My sister came looking for me because we always went home together. I was crying and she got real angry with the teacher. She said that our mother didn't hit us at home so she had no business hitting me in school. The teacher took me into the washroom, washed my face and gave me her handkerchief and after that she was great friends with us and walked home with us every day. I liked going to St. Dominic's. We had nice people there. The school was divided with sliding doors, the boys on one side and the girls on the other.

Father Flanagan was a very nice priest. All the girls used to flock around him. He used to come to the school and give a lecture every Tuesday afternoon. We spent a lot of time in St. Dominic's Church. We'd go for choir practice and we kept the holy days and we had to go to the nine o'clock Mass every Sunday and if we couldn't tell the sister the gospel we had to write lines.

I remember our first radio. It was a crystal set that my father made. It was a little box with a crystal and it had a needle and you had to work it around on this crystal to get the station. We had to put on earphones to hear the programs and you hooked the earphones on to this little box. I think we had two sets of earphones. When we got our first real radio you had to have a radio licence. It cost two dollars, I think, and they used to send people around to check and ask if you had a radio. My mother always used to warn me, "If you go to the door and it's the inspector for the radio licence just tell him you have one. If he wants to see it tell him you don't know where it is right now." But they'd always insist; they'd want to see the licence.

My father was very strict and we weren't allowed to go out with boys until we were sixteen. I always had lots of boyfriends but my sister was the beauty in the family and she always stole my boyfriends. (laughs) They'd go out with me and I'd bring them home and the next thing I knew they were phoning her for a date. We had a curfew. Even if we went to parties we had to be in at eleven o'clock. The first thing my father wanted to know about any boy we went out with was his religion. I remember going with one fellow for a long time and my father never spoke to him because he wasn't an RC. That's the way we were brought up. In those days it was either right or wrong, black or white, there was no in-between. We were always allowed to bring our friends home and have parties. We used to take down the beds in one room to give us space and we had a wind-up gramophone. One would bring cakes and someone else would bring sandwiches or drinks or something. Then somebody else would have a party the next week. When my sister and I got older we used to go to dances at the Grenadier Guards. Of course we got home later then but the boys we went with were friends of the family who belonged to the Guards so it was all right. My parents knew them and they knew we'd get home safely.

I think I was sixteen when I got my first job at a company called Semi-Ready. I addressed envelopes and sent out samples of material for men's suits. I got about six dollars a week but of course you could get a pair of shoes for two dollars and a dress for two or three dollars. A nickel went a lot further than it does today. Then I went to work for the Northern. A friend told me that I would get a job at the Northern because my name was Murphy and the man hiring was an O'Brien. That's where I met my future husband.

The Depression affected our family. Things like sugar and tea were scarce. I remember we used to dry out the tea bags and use them again. Hamburger and sausages used to be a cheap meal in those days. That's what you ate if you didn't have much money or you'd get a bone and make a big pot of soup. We always had food on the table though and my parents paid the bills. We never got too many new clothes or new furniture but we ate well enough. My father always had a job.

I got married in 1942 to James Neville. My husband's father was born in County Wexford. The Graneys, his mother's side also came from Ireland but I don't know which part. The war was on when we got married but my husband didn't go because his heart wasn't too strong. A lot of my friends, boys that I grew up with, went and never returned. It makes you feel sad.

My first son was born in Rosemount and then in 1947 we went to live in Point St. Charles. My husband's parents lived there and they had a property on D'Argenson so we moved into one of the flats and my other four sons were born there and went to Canon O'Meara School.

Raising five boys I never had much time to myself. I was always busy but that was my world. I enjoyed looking after them and trying to see that they did the right thing. I tried to bring them up to be good, decent citizens. If they'd fight I'd gather them around me and I'd say, "This is your brother, your flesh and blood. When you hit him you might as well be hitting yourself because he has the same flesh and blood as you do." They used to have their little scraps but there's one thing—if one of them went out and somebody picked on him, all the others would go out and stand up for that brother and nobody dared touch him.

Taking them out was always an adventure. I'd get them all dressed up for church and by the time I got the last one ready I'd have to start on the first one again because he was down in the yard getting dirty. When we got to church we'd have to separate them because they'd start pinching each other and giggling and I'd have to sit between them the same as when we went in the car. I never got to sit in the front because I had to stay in the back to keep order and keep them from teasing each other. But it was lots of fun.

I was house proud in that I wanted everything neat and clean but my children were allowed to bring their friends home. They would play in the house and I'd bake three or four times a week and make them cookies and cupcakes and all kinds of stuff like that. When it was their birthdays, each one had a party and a cake. When they were older we used to have a party every New Year's Eve and they always invited their friends. On the weekends I never knew who was sleeping over. I'd get up on Saturday morning and there'd be bodies all over the place lying on the floor.

It wasn't an easy life bringing up the boys but I enjoyed it. I used to tell them that they made me laugh more than they made me cry so I guess that was the main thing. I also had a good husband. I don't think he ever said an unkind word to me all the years we were married. I never saw him lose his temper and, bringing up the boys, he left everything to me. He'd say, "Go and ask your mother."

My husband died in 1968. We had just moved to Verdun so the boys would be able to go to Verdun Catholic High. I never thought when they were growing up that some day we would be separated. I never thought that their father would pass away and leave me while they were still in school. Jimmy had just started to work in the Northern and the other four were in high school. Patrick was about thirteen.

I live with Susan and Denis and I still keep busy. I don't know how people can say they're bored. There's always something to do and I'm never bored. It's always open house here and we still have plenty of company. I tell everybody that the door is always open and if they want to come, they're welcome. There's always a meal and cookies and cakes on the table.

I'd do it all over again. The years have passed so quickly; one day your children are babies and the next thing you know they're grown up and gone. We're still close. We visit, we talk on the phone and get together whenever we can. I brought them up to always be close to one another. I told them, "Family counts. Always stick together and look after one another."

I know I'm getting older. I'm not afraid of dying but I don't want to go and leave my loved ones behind. That's the only thing; leaving them behind, but I hope when I do go I'll be able to watch over them.

Patricia Mullally

Patricia Mullally was born in Montreal in 1911. She is the daughter of Dr. Emmett J. Mullally, one of the more prominent members of the Irish-Canadian Catholic community during the first half of this century. Dr. Mullally was a physician, an author and an educator. Patricia Mullally worked for many years for the Red Cross (Veterans' Services) and later the RCAFBF (Royal Canadian Air Force Benevolent Fund). She was also active in many volunteer organizations, such as the St. Mary's Auxiliary and the Catholic Women's League.

My father was born in Souris, Prince Edward Island. There was an Irishman in his town who had made a lot of money. He never married and established a scholarship. My father won it and came to McGill to study medicine. The scholarship, if I remember rightly, was $250 a year on which to live and pay your fees. When my father was at McGill, there was no place for Catholic students to meet. He was one of the many Catholic students who decided to form what was later called the Columbian Club.* Monsignor McShane, who was Father McShane in those days, became its first chaplain. It was a very active organization and later became known as the Newman Club.

It was always my father's habit, when he went to another city, to look in the directory to see if there were any other Mullallys in the book. He discovered that there was a Mullally family on Papineau Square. He was a great walker and he used to walk down to Papineau Square from where he was living to see if he could catch a glimpse of these Mullallys. (laughs) It was just a question of curiosity. I don't recall how he actually met the family but through some way of his he managed to meet my mother. They didn't start courting each other at that stage but I think they were both interested in the fact that they had the same name because Mullally is not a common name. Eventually, they married in 1906 and so Mother married a Mullally and never changed her name.

Being a Roman Catholic and of Irish descent, my father could work at a French hospital because they were Catholic. The Royal Victoria and the Montreal General Hospital were the only two English-speaking hospitals and my father was actually accepted by the Royal Victoria Hospital as a "houseman" as interns were called then. He graduated in 1901 at the age of twenty-three and from 1901 until 1903 he interned there, which was quite a feather in his cap. In 1903 he began practicing medicine. He never talked openly about the prejudice he must have felt but I can recall that there must have been a certain amount of it.

My maternal grandfather, James E. Mullally, came over from Ireland with his father at around the age of thirteen and eventually founded a cartage business of his own in which he became very successful. There were horse-drawn carts in those days and I can remember the stables behind the house. By the time we were born, I think my grandfather had retired. My mother was an only child and when she and my father were first married they had a flat on Park Avenue near my father's office but they came back to live in my grandparent's large house at 63 Papineau Square and the six children that they had were born there. Papineau Square was in the eastern part of Montreal at the end of Papineau Street below Dorchester (now René Lévesque). When I was a kid growing up in my grandmother's house there used to be a military cemetery on the east side of Papineau above St. Catherine Street.**

My father was the doctor for the Dominion Rubber Company which was on Craig Street and he also saw patients at 63 Papineau Square. It was a large house. My grandmother had a double parlour on the main floor, a front parlour and a back parlour. Beside that was a room at the end of the hall where my father had his office. Eventually, we moved further west when my father bought a property on Union Avenue above what was Burnside then and is now de Maisonneuve. At that time, Union Avenue was referred to as the Harley Street of Montreal because there were several doctors who had residences on that street. Next door to our house was Dr. DeJersey White who was connected with the Royal Victoria Hospital. Dr. Frank McKenty, (also a Catholic) who was the surgeon-in-chief at the Royal Victoria, also lived on our street.

My father was a past-president of St. Patrick's Society and a member of the Catholic School Commission. He was very anxious to bring out the qualities of the English-speaking, Irish-Canadian Catholics and show what they could do. He felt that they weren't given enough prominence in the community. Many of the meetings of the Catholic School Commission were held in French and, of course, the French you learn on Prince Edward Island is very minimal but he had enough to understand what was going on. The chairman of the school commission at that time was Mr. Victor Doré who was a very fine man and very sympathetic to my father's causes. As a result of my father's devotion to those Catholics of Irish descent, he was instrumental in having the first English-Catholic high school for boys and girls (under the Catholic School Commission) established which he named D'Arcy McGee High School.

As a youth in a country school in Souris my father learned McGee's poem, "Jacques Cartier." My father became very enchanted with McGee and his poems at a very early age so he decided he was going to do something to let the people know about Thomas McGee and his contribution to Canadian society. After all, he was a Father of Confederation but little was known about him except that he had represented Montreal West and had been assassinated. This became a life-long interest of my father's which is why he had the school named after McGee. McGee's daughter Agnes was alive at the time and he had many an interview with her about her father and he eventually wrote many articles on McGee and his achievements.

My father had a lot on his platter. He was also a president of the St. James's Literary Society, chairman of the medical board of St. Mary's Hospital, president-general of the Canadian Catholic Historical Association, a member of the Board of Governors of Catholic High School, a warden of St. Patrick's Parish and medical advisor of the St. Patrick's Orphanage. During World War I, he was a lieutenant and medical officer for the Irish Rangers. I have a book that shows pictures of him and Lieutenant Colonel Trihey and Captain Weir. There were many other names in Montreal that were connected with the Irish Rangers.

One interesting aspect of my father was that he experimented in teaching with my two youngest sisters. He decided to teach them at home so every morning at the breakfast table we'd see Ben (Brenda) and Jean getting their lessons from my father. He'd be taking their lessons and giving them work to do. My mother used to say, "Emmett, you're ruining those children. They won't know how to behave when they get to school." But anyway, he persisted and they both did very well. He gave us all lessons and was a great teacher. My sisters were sufficiently well educated so that they met the requirements to enter second year high at D'Arcy McGee, his newly-established high school.

My sister Eileen and I had a private teacher, a lady by the name of Frankie (Frances) McCabe. She was a very charming lady who used to come to the house and give us lessons. Jessie, the eldest in the family had gone to the Sacred Heart on St. Alexander Street and then to St. Urbain Academy which was in an old private home on St. Urbain Street above Prince Arthur. It had lovely grounds and a circular driveway. Eileen and I went there to make our First Communion but, apart from that, we had lessons at home until we went to the Sacred Heart. I started off in what they called third preparatory, the year before high school and then I went into high school.

The Sacred Heart was a lovely school. They had quite a different system. In the morning you assembled in what they called the study hall. You had your desk there where you kept all your books. Then you went to general class when the bell rang. You lined up as a class together and then you marched solemnly (laughs) out to your classroom. You had other teachers for mathematics and

French. We had a navy blue uniform with a Peter Pan collar and cuffs which were the deuce to keep clean, I can tell you. (laughs) The uniform had tucks and a pleated skirt. You had pockets where you could easily put the odd candy but they were meant to carry a hanky. They had a beautiful chapel in the convent and the boys from Collège Ste-Marie were just across the street and they would act as altar boys when the priest came from the Collège to say Mass. We could also watch all the boys playing over there, you know. (laughs)

We used to have house parties when we lived on Union Avenue and had this large room upstairs where we'd hold them. We'd clear the room of furniture so there was room for 20-25 people to dance. We had always wanted a gramophone but Mother had refused to get one because she wanted us to devote our time to our music. Finally, we got one in the thirties. These parties were all very innocent in a sense. There was no liquor. We had sandwiches and soft drinks or coffee or tea, that sort of thing. It was all very interesting. People seemed to like coming to the house because they always came back. We also used to go to parties where there was a pianist. You know, one of the crowd who was a good pianist would play and you'd dance and have a singsong.

When I became older, in my early twenties, I'd go to the St. Patrick's Society Ball at the Windsor Hotel which was a very posh affair in those days—I imagine it still is. The men would wear tails and the women would wear formal ball gowns. I can remember, too, as a little girl, Mother getting ready to go to the St. Patrick's Ball. She would get a special dress made and go off with my father in his tails. They made a very handsome couple.

Mother was very artistic. She attended the Academy of St. Denis where she took art lessons. All the paintings you see in this house are hers and some of them were painted even after the doctors discovered she had leukemia. She was really only able to return to painting after my youngest sister was old enough to look after herself. When the Catholic Women's League held a competition to choose an emblem to represent the league, Mother won the competition. The emblem has a black cross on a blue background and underneath the cross there are maple leaves representing each province of Canada. At the time there were nine and they added another when Newfoundland came in. Mother also wrote some articles on art in Canada and gave a few talks although she was a very shy woman and it made her nervous to address the public. She never told us her age. She was very proud about that. You'd ask her and she'd say, "I'm 102." She was probably two or three years older than my father which might have been the reason.

(top) Patricia Mullally's mother (right), circa 1900, standing outside
her parents' house at 63 Papineau Square.
(bottom) The Mullally children in 1921. (left to right) Jessie,
Jimmy, Patricia, Eileen, Brenda (Ben) and Jean
Photos courtesy of Patricia Mullally.

My parents were both very Irish. So much so that, much to our embarrassment, if we went to the movies with Mother and they played "God Save the King," she just sat. She wouldn't stand and we used to say, "Mother, stand up. Everybody else is." "I am not going to stand up," she'd say. She wasn't going to stand up for "God Save the King." After all, her father had come from Ireland, although he was young when he came.

One of my father's friends had a housekeeper and governess, Miss Kennedy. She taught the children at home and, after they grew up, she decided to open a business school. She was an excellent teacher so Eileen and I were sent to Miss Kennedy to take a business course. I worked for the Red Cross for many years and found it most interesting work. I was in charge of the department which dealt with veterans. It was the beginning of the war, 1939, and we looked after veterans of the First World War who needed financial assistance until they received their first pay from the service. We were able to help them through the Poppy Day Fund which were funds collected on Armistice Day each year.

Dr. Donald Hingston, who was one of the founders of St. Mary's Hospital, had five daughters. Katherine, one of his daughters, was a contemporary of mine and we had been at the Sacred Heart Convent together. Katherine and I worked together in the St. Mary's Auxiliary. We used to go up when they opened the hospital on Lacombe and roll bandages and do things for the surgery department. Of course, many friendships were made through the Auxiliary—lasting friendships at that, too.

I was one of the founders, along with now Bishop Crowley, (who was then a curate at St. Patrick's) of the St. Patrick's Women's Club. They had a very active Unity Club for the men and an outstanding choir for men only. My brother Jimmy was a choir boy and he used to wear Eton suits which are so cute. Monsignor McShane (who married my parents) was a very fine man but he didn't believe, or so I'm told, in having women's groups other than the Sodality. We had a very successful women's club and we raised an awful lot of money for the church. We'd have a three-day bazaar and Florence Hackett always looked after the suppers. If people didn't come to anything else, they'd come for the meal so we were very successful in raising a fair amount of money for the church. Monsignor Doran (who was the pastor) was very happy with the club but when Monsignor Dubee took over the parish he decided he didn't want any money-making activities so that was the end of the St. Patrick's Women's Club. We did a lot for the church.

St. Patrick's Day was always great. Union Avenue was a wide street, one of the widest in the area so parades coming along Sherbrooke Street would turn down Union. The St. Patrick's Society was the last in the parade and my father, Dr. Donnelly and some other men were usually in the last row. All the grandchildren called my father Goggy because they couldn't pronounce grandfather. They all came down to Union Avenue to watch Goggy in the parade. One time, it was a beautiful, sunny day and my father, of course, always looked over to the house. The children were on the stairs and, as soon as they spotted my father they all dashed down to him and said, "Oh, Goggy", and started walking with him down to the end of the parade. (laughs) It was the cutest thing to see.

Our house on Union Avenue was expropriated by the city in 1960 and my father, Eileen and I moved to Melbourne Avenue in Westmount. Mother had died the previous year, in 1959. She would have loved the new house. (Both she and my father died in their eighties.)

---

*In 1898, Edward Devine, S.J. gathered a group of Catholic McGill students together and this became the nucleus of The Loyola Club of McGill University. Emmett Mullally was one of the first officers of this club in 1898. In 1902, Father Devine opened a club house at the corner of Dorchester and St. Genevieve Streets but this venture was short-lived when Father Devine was sent on a mission to Alaska causing the end of the Loyola Club. Two years later, Father Gerald McShane was asked to become chaplain of the former Loyola Club. The name Columbian Club evolved due to the fact that early meetings of the club were held in the chambers of the Canada Council of the Knights of Columbus then located at the corner of Sherbrooke Street and Park Avenue. The Columbian Club became the Newman Club in 1929. (Source: *Loyola and Montreal, A History* by T.P. Slattery, Montreal, Palm Publishers, 1962.)

**The military cemetery was moved in the 1920s after many of the graves had been vandalized. The bodies were then interred in the Field of Honour in Point Claire. One of the bodies buried in the original military cemetery was Sir Benjamin D'Urban, a British general and colonial administrator whose treatment of the Africans when he served as governor in the Cape Colony in the early nineteenth century so disturbed some elements of the British colony that he was dismissed as governor in 1838 but continued as commander-in-chief until 1846. In 1847 he took up command of the British forces in Canada and died at Montreal in 1849. Durban, the largest city of Natal, South Africa was named after him.

Terence Finn

Wrestling has been one of Terry Finn's lifelong interests. He started wrestling when he was eighteen or nineteen years old and he won the Provincial Championship in 1935. For many years he came into Montreal from his home in Greenfield Park to practice his sport at the downtown "Y" where he often ran into his old friend Frank Hanley. He was born in England in 1912 and came to Canada soon after. He has many stories to tell of the severe discipline doled out by the Presentation Brothers.

My birthday is November 30th which, as I understand it, is the feast of the patron saint of Scotland, St. Andrew. I was born in England. My mother's family came from Tipperary and my dad's family came from Cork and I suppose that they moved to England at the time of the potato famine. My mother was actually born in Siam (Thailand) in 1884. She was a Donovan and the story is that her father had been invited by a missionary to go to Siam to tutor some of the members of the royal family. He spent four or five years there and we still have my mother's birth certificate. My father's people in England still have little mementos that my grandfather was given by the King of Siam. Being born in England meant that, later on, when I travelled to the States with friends, I would have to tell the border guards where I was born and everybody would start calling out, "You bloody Limey."

My dad came from a place not too far from Wimbledon. He had six sisters and when he was ten or twelve, his mother decided that he should be a priest. I understand that the same thing used to happen in French-Canadian families too. He was educated by the Franciscans and then went to study at St. Peter and St. Paul's Seminary in Portugal. He stayed until he was twenty-four or twenty-five years old. The story is that he wasn't too well and the priest in charge of the seminary suggested that he leave because, "No man's life was more miserable than a priest who couldn't say Mass because of sickness."

I was only six months old when we moved to Canada in 1913, a year after the sinking of the *Titanic*. My dad came first and my mother followed with the children which included my older sister Moira, my brother James, another older sister Catherine and me. We landed in Halifax and went to Toronto where my father was working at the Post Office. War broke out in 1914 and Dad decided to sign up with a Toronto regiment. He was the only boy of seven children and I imagine he thought it was a great chance to go back and visit his sisters. Everyone thought that the war would be over within a month or two but it didn't happen that way. He was gassed at Ypres* and returned home in

1916, I believe. He then went up to a sanatorium at Muskoka Lake which treated people with lung troubles. We lived in Gravenhurst and Bracebridge while my dad was in and out of the sanatorium. When he was a little better he returned to the Post Office and decided to come to Montreal so we came here in 1919. He worked all his life at Station A, the main Post Office on St. James Street.

We lived way up in Ahuntsic on Lajeunesse Street near Cremazie. We were about half a mile from the Back River. There weren't too many English people there and I made my First Communion in French at St. Alphonse de Youville Church as did my older brother and my two sisters. As a matter of fact, I used to go to Confession in French and say my Act of Contrition in French, too. I didn't even know it in English. I was bilingual to a certain extent but then I got away from it until we moved to Point St. Charles. The whole area of Ahuntsic had wide-open spaces and there was a Jewish cemetery nearby. We could actually see Bordeaux Jail and whenever they would hang a prisoner they would raise a black flag that same morning.

I went to St. Michael's School on Boucher Street off St. Denis in the north end of the city. We had the Marist Brothers and I only stayed for one year. Then my dad bought a piece of property and had a house built in East Greenfield which is now a part of St. Hubert. We were there until about 1923. The funny thing about the piece of land that my dad bought was that there was no road leading to it. (laughs) You had to go through the fields. There were four of us going to school. My sisters went to school in St. Lambert for a year and then went to St. Patrick's. My brother and I went to St. Ann's in Griffintown and we had to commute every day. We'd have to get up and catch the train at a quarter to eight and if you missed that one you had to wait until eleven o'clock. I don't remember us ever missing the train, though. It was hard going to a school that was not in our neighbourhood. There was a Protestant school that we could have gone to but my dad said, "No, you can't go there because in England and Ireland you weren't allowed to go to a Protestant school." He wouldn't hear of us going to it and it was right close by. No way would he allow us to go.

While we were living there a very sad thing happened. There were two boys at home, Donal and Desmond, who were babies at the time. My poor mother boiled some water one day to do some washing and Desmond got scalded when the pail of water got knocked over. He had a sweater on and it got soaked. She had to sit from ten in the morning until six at night until somebody arrived home and the next day the poor little fellow died. The closest doctor had to come in from St. Lambert. We left East Greenfield right after that and moved to

Soulanges Street in Point St. Charles.

There was a gentleman who had brought ten donkeys over from Ireland and was charging people five or ten cents a ride on St. Helen's Island. It didn't work out too well so my dad bought one of the donkeys for seventy-five dollars which included the saddle. We took it from Montreal to East Greenfield and it came with us to Soulanges Street. We had to put it in a stable which was just next door but the novelty soon wore off and we got tired of the donkey. It was a shaggy thing and all the kids thought it was a nanny goat. My dad decided, seeing that we weren't interested in it any more, that he would give it to St. Patrick's Orphanage. A good friend of mine, John Moore, was in St. Patrick's at that time and the nuns appointed him to look after the donkey. I had been in school with John and he later became a policeman but every time I see him he curses me up and down because it was on account of me and my family that he got stuck with the donkey and had to clean up after it.

I was eleven when we moved to Point St. Charles and then I went to St. Gabriel's School. There is a famous story about Brother Edmund, the fourth grade teacher, who was 6'2" and weighed about 240 pounds. I even heard this story from my mother. They say that if you didn't study he would grab you by the scruff of the neck, open the window and hold you out and ask, "Are you going to study?" He'd hold you out until you said yes and then he'd bring you back in. That story.....he must have done that to ten or twenty thousand people. Just not possible.** One thing about Brother Edmund though—he had this big ruler and if you made mistakes in spelling or grammar, he'd hold your left hand and rap you across the knuckles. There were about thirty-five boys in the class and our knuckles were blue all week. By Saturday they'd get a little better but on Monday you'd start all over again. There was one boy named Holland who rarely got hit but the rest of us....he'd give us five Catechism questions to memorize and if you missed the one he asked you then you got your punishment. He used to ask us to spell "bow" so you'd spell b-o-w and you got hit. Next student, "How do you spell "bow"?" He'd say b-o-u-g-h and get hit. After going through the whole class he'd say, "You're supposed to ask *which* bow." He was very strict and we were afraid of him. One of my aunts or my grandmother used to send my dad a newspaper from Cork every month and the whole class would look forward to Terry Finn bringing in the Irish paper and giving it to Brother Edmund because he would sit there and read and things would be quiet for a while. (laughs) We were assured that we weren't going to get the old ruler for an hour or so. This same brother was also in charge of the choir. He'd bring you in and ask you to sing a few notes and, good or bad, you were in the choir. Sometimes, after lunch, as we would line up to go in, he'd be on the first landing and call you in for a meeting and keep you there for about fifteen minutes. Then, when you got up to your floor, you'd be late and Brother Rogers, the director was waiting for you. "How come you're late?" (laughs) So you just couldn't win.

This Brother Rogers was also called Brother Sebastian. He was a huge man and he was the boss. When he blew the whistle at the end of recess, we had to freeze in whatever position we were in and ten seconds later he'd blow the whistle again and you ran as fast as you could to line up. He sure scared the hell out of us. When I was in fifth or sixth grade, I had a teacher who was a brilliant man and an excellent teacher. His name was Brother Finbar and he had whiskers. He was one of the original twenty-five Presentation Brothers who came here from Ireland. He was as gentle as could be and wouldn't touch anybody as far as punishment was concerned. Once, just before Christmas, we were coming downstairs and a couple of fellows were talking. Brother Rogers heard this, walked over, stopped everybody and said to poor Brother Finbar, "O.K. Whiskers. I'll take over." Brother Finbar left and we all went back to class. It was nearly four o'clock and he told us to get out our grammar books and study and that he would come back in half an hour. When he came back he asked us a question. There were only two who knew the answer and the rest of us had to line up and we got the strap. He kept asking questions and if you knew the answer you sat down. If you didn't know it you got the strap. We sat there until about five o'clock. A woman came in looking for her son and he said, "Want your son? Here. Don't come back." In those days we never heard of complaining to the school board. We hadn't even heard about a school board! We thought he was the boss and sure enough—when we came back after the holidays, Brother Finbar was gone and we had a new teacher, Brother Bonaventure. One thing I always feel sad about was that I never visited Brother Finbar when he was in the Presentation Brothers' retirement home in Longeuil, not far from where I live.

About fifteen years ago, I read in the paper that Brother Rogers had passed away. I went to Longeuil to pay my respects and there was nobody around. A brother came and saw me and showed me where to go and there was Brother Rogers laid out, still about 6'3" and looking as tough and stern as ever. I didn't understand and I don't approve of how strict some of them were but certainly, for education and learning, you couldn't beat them. I've never forgotten the prayers and poems that I was taught. One of my sons who had a Catholic education was never sure of his prayers. I certainly appreciate, too, all the things they taught us in religion class.

Brother Joseph was a great man. He used to flood the hockey rink at the side of the school on Laprairie Street. Ten below zero or whatever the temperature he was out there flooding the rink with his bare hands. We had a hockey team and we had to practice at seven in the morning. This would have been 1926-1927. I think it must have been a midget team, sixteen or under. We played against other Catholic schools and we got into the playoffs which were held at the Forum that year. St. Gabriel's won that particular championship. One of the boys on that team was Johnny Taugher, Percy's brother and another one was Gerald Mullins.

We all tried to get out of the choir because we always had to go to eleven o'clock Mass, which was always a High Mass. It would finish at 12:30 and then we had choir practice for an hour. The organist was a lady by the name of Mrs. Monaghan and we'd be there until 1:30 or twenty to two. Most of the other kids would go somewhere in the afternoon but we couldn't so the big thing was how to get out of the choir and there was no way with this Brother Edmund in charge. I'm happy today that I had that training although I'm not a great singer.

One of the things I can recall back in the 1920s when we lived in Point St. Charles were the stockyards which were close to Canada Packers on Bridge Street. In those days they had to take the cattle across the street to the slaughterhouse. Years after they had an overpass built but before that, when the animals would cross the street, some steer would get away and run down Bridge Street and land up in somebody's back yard. Then the police would be called to rope the animal. We also had the Belding Corticelli boxing club which produced some good boxers like Harold Stewart who was on the Olympic team in 1928. Another good boxer was Johnny Keller, a Polish boy. By 1934-1935 it closed and was turned into a cafeteria. Today it is a condo complex.

We moved from Point St. Charles over to Chatham Street near St. Antoine which is in what we used to call the West End. I was an altar boy so I kept going back to serve Mass at St. Gabriel's. In those days it was an honour to be an altar boy and you would do it until you were about twenty-two or twenty-three years old. We had people working who were still on the altar, you know.

I was one of the fortunate ones. In 1930, on St. Patrick's Day, I got a job in the CNR Cartage at the famous salary of ten dollars a week. You worked six days a week but I was lucky to have a job during the Depression and I stayed there until 1938. I wasn't married then and was still living at home with my parents.

I had a brother living in Hamilton and I decided my fortune was there so I resigned and moved to Ontario. I stayed with my brother but it was 1938 and things were no better there. I wound up getting eighteen cents an hour working for E.D. Smith. I stayed there until I had enough money to come back to Montreal because I didn't want to ask my parents for the money. It took me about a year to get organized again. I did little jobs and in 1941 I was fortunate again because I started working for Canadian Oil, better known as White Rose. In those days they were on Bridge Street, of all places, so it was back to Griffintown. I stayed at Canadian Oil for a few years. I went on the road as a salesman and then was made purchasing agent. In 1950 I was asked to go to Toronto as one of the buyers in the Purchasing Department. Two years later, in 1951, I was made assistant purchasing agent.

I married Gisèle Laberge in June of 1953. I was forty going on forty-one but you know the Irish. I think one of the reasons I married late was that we had the Depression and no way could you afford to get married and then the war came along. Many of the people I knew got married in their thirties. In 1949 while I was at Canadian Oil, this young, fully bilingual young lady came in as a secretary from the Mother House. Gisèle stayed there for two years and then decided to go into nursing so she left the company and went to St. Mary's Hospital for her training. We were married right after she graduated. I was still in Toronto and our two daughters, Julia Patricia and Cathy, were born there. I was transferred back to Montreal and Sean, Patrick and Michelle were born here. Julia's a librarian for the Department of Indian Affairs, Cathy works for a pharmaceutical company. Sean is a senior vice-president of CNR and is married to a French girl. He's probably more French than English. Patrick is a naval officer and Michelle graduated in biology from the Université de Montréal.

A friend of mine said that anyone who grew up in Point St. Charles was bilingual before Bill 101 because we all spoke a certain amount of French. We may have murdered the language but we were never afraid of it. I make a habit, if I'm at the YMCA, to speak French if I know the other fellow is French. They probably speak better English than I do. They are all lawyers and what not. I think it's a two-way street. I certainly don't see a problem at all.

I've been very fortunate. I'm in my eighties and I've only been in the hospital once for a very minor thing. I always say that God doesn't close a window unless He opens a door and vice versa.

*There were three Battles of Ypres during the Great War but the battle of April-May, 1915 was notable because it was the first time that the Germans used poison gas.

**This story about a brother who suspended boys out of a window is also told about St. Ann's Boys' School. It keeps cropping up with some saying that it never happened and others swearing that it did. One thing it does indicate is that discipline was very tough indeed and it was always a wise move for a boy to study hard and behave himself.

An important day for the Finn family—Terry, Moira, Catherine, and James—on the occasion of Terry's First Communion and his siblings' Confirmation in 1919. *Courtesy of Terry Finn.*

Lieutenant John Moore

John (Jack) Moore was born in 1914 in New Aberdeen, Cape Breton Island, Nova Scotia, but moved to Montreal with his parents and brothers and sisters when he was eight years old. Tragedy struck the family soon after their arrival in Montreal when his father was killed in an accident and Jack and his brother Raphael were placed in St. Patrick's Orphanage. His brother never adjusted to orphanage life but for Jack, it was a positive experience which he remembers fondly. Active in many organizations, he used to take part in the plays put on by St. Gabriel's Parish, once playing the playboy in "The Playboy of the Western World." Jack Moore spent twenty-eight years on the Montreal Police Force, from 1936 until 1964.

My parents were born in Newfoundland, my mother in St. John's and my dad in Kelligrews. There's a story about Kelligrews. They always said that the place where my father was born was so healthy they had to shoot a tourist to start a cemetery. I was born in New Aberdeen, Nova Scotia. The family moved to Montreal when I was around eight years old. We lived in Verdun at first and then moved to Congregation Street in the Point. I had five brothers and three sisters. My sister Kathleen's father-in-law was Johnny Maloney, the great Irish piano player.

My dad was killed shortly after we moved to Montreal in a railroad accident. It was Easter Sunday morning. He had just left St. Gabriel's Church where he received Holy Communion. Twenty minutes after he made his Easter duty he was killed. He was a yard man for the CNR and he got caught between two freight cars. Then I was sent to St. Patrick's Orphanage and spent two years up there. My brother Raphael, who passed away a few years ago, and I were sent there and the others stayed at home. The canon in charge of the parish of St. Gabriel's was a great friend of my father and, as there were too many of us at home, he made the decision to put two of us in the orphanage. I wasn't solicited whether I wanted to go or not, I was just sent.

I loved it at the orphanage. They were good years, happy years. When I first went in I was lonely because we were a big family but, after a while, I got used to it. The Grey Nuns were very good to me. There were two section in the orphanage, one for girls and one for boys. I think we were about sixty boys. The food was good but I can tell you one incident: I was captain of a table and this new kid called Meaney came in. We became good friends later on. We were having porridge for breakfast and he said: "I don't like porridge." I said: "You'd better eat it." He said that he didn't eat porridge so the nun took the plate, put it away and we went to school. We came back at dinner and he was given the porridge. I said: "You better eat it." He said: "No, I don't like it."They took the plate away and he had it again for supper. Then he ate it. (laughs) I said, "If you don't eat it, that's the only plate you're going to get. You can't get anything else unless you eat it."You had to have some kind of discipline with so many children. You can't say, "I don't want this." or "I want that."

We never mingled with the girls—we didn't go up in that section. There was also a section for crib babies on the second floor. I worked in the laundry. They had a huge laundry and I worked on the mangle. I would put the sheets through the mangle. The nuns also taught us how to darn our socks. I had no complaints whatsoever. There was a classroom upstairs and we were taught by the nuns. Later on in life when I was working as a policeman, I used to discuss the orphanage with one or two other policemen who had also been there and they had no complaints either. My brother, Raphael, however, didn't take to it too well and they sent him home. He was a problem up there. He was two years younger than me and he couldn't handle it. He refused everything and stayed alone all the time until my mother came and took him home.

Terry Finn lived in St. Gabriel's Parish and his mother and father somehow acquired a donkey and, since they didn't have a stable they donated it to the orphanage. Sister Lamarre, who was in charge of our division, appointed me as the donkey's guardian. I had to go and take him from the barn, bring him to the orchard, bring him back to the barn and clean up the barn. I cursed that donkey and Terry Finn and his family from here to Ireland. (laughs) The donkey was still there when I left and I don't know what happened to it.

I didn't have too much schooling. I came out of the orphanage when I was eleven and had finished sixth grade. I went to McGee with five other fellows from St. Gabriel's as football players and when the football season was over they threw us all out. We were all six footers and were brought up to McGee by this American brother. After we won the championship we were just eased out of the school. That was it. (laughs) We were ringers brought in from the Point. Presence no longer required unless we could have made the hockey team but none of us were hockey players. Some of the fellows who went up with me were George Nichol who became the divisional chief of the Montreal Fire Department, Leo Kearney who later started his own insurance business, Jimmy McCrory who got the DFC overseas, and Jimmy Conway. They've all passed away.

Father Reid was the chaplain when I first went to the orphanage and after him it was Father O'Reilly. When Father O'Reilly left the orphanage he was sent to

St. Gabriel's. It was around the time that I came back home. Since I knew him, he had me running his messages and serving Mass and Benediction so I was always associated with St. Gabriel's Parish. In fact, he was the one who got me on the Police Force. He was a great friend of Senator Hushion. Hogan was the alderman at the time and he had another boy lined up for the Police Force but he couldn't pass the medical so they tried another boy but he didn't pass either. Father O'Reilly got hold of Hushion and Hushion got hold of Hogan and Hogan got hold of me and I went down and I passed the medical. There wasn't a scholastic test, if you were healthy you were hired. It was in 1936 and I was in my early twenties. I studied at the Police Academy on Ontario Street East. The training lasted three months and then I was sent right back to the Point as a young cop.

While I was in training I got called down to headquarters and the secretary to the director said to me, "You signed the form saying that you speak French." I said, "Yes." He said, "You don't speak French." I said, "No." So he said, "We'll have to let you go." So Senator Hushion came down and said, "That's O.K. Let him go. He can't speak French but tomorrow morning every boy who's French and who can't speak English should be gone too." They sent me back. I never had any trouble after that. I don't ever remember seeing any trouble between the French and the English. Some of my best friends in the police department are French Canadians and we still meet and go out together for lunch or a drink. I had enough French to understand what was going on and when I became an officer and went out on a call I always had someone in the radio car with me who could speak both languages fluently.

Those were tough times, you know. People were hungry and there was no work. It was right in the deep Depression. People were getting seventeen cents an hour and CNR wages were twenty-five cents an hour. People were desperate. My mother and my brother Leo counselled me to become a policeman. I was told, "You'd better take it because there's nothing. You're not going to get work anywhere." Police work gave us a certain amount of security and our uniforms were supplied. Transportation was supplied too so we had no problems in that area. My first beat was Goose Village. The people were good to us, especially the Italian people who lived there. They'd call you into their grocery stores and make you a sandwich and give you a bottle of milk. Things were very tough. I made five dollars a week and you can't do much with that. That was my pay and I worked thirteen hours a night and you got one day off every three weeks. (laughs) If a strike broke out, then you didn't get your day off. You had to work and there was no such thing as saying, "It's my day off, I'm going home." No, no, you had to work.

There were a lot of Irish policemen in those days. When I reported down in the Point, there was an Irish Captain, John O'Neill. Number 10 had Captain Corbett. Captain Minogue was up in N.D.G. The head of the Detective Office was William Fitzpatrick. Leo Murray was head of correspondence. Earl McGrath had a big job as a detective with the Police Department. But today the Irish are all gone from the police department. It seems that all I do now is go to funerals. All the Irish boys who joined up with me, Emmet Hayes, Toddy Cartwright, Sonny Nolan, Buddy Clark, Bill Robinson, John Ranson and John Heffernan have all passed away.

We reported to the station at six o'clock in the evening. The beats would start; 7 to 10, 10 to 1, 1 to 4, and 4 to 7. You were three hours out and three hours in. You had your own bed in the dormitory upstairs where you slept and then they woke you up to go back on the beat. There were about thirty or forty beds. If you didn't want to sleep, you played cards. We put in six hours on the beat and six hours at the station. Actually you spent thirteen hours in there. The day shift was from seven in the morning till six in the evening but we only went on days about once every five or six months. We didn't get too much day work. You had to walk your beat and you went from box to box. You had twenty minutes between each box. When you pulled the lever it registered in the station on a tape and if you missed a box they'd send somebody out to hunt for you. There were no radio cars in the mid-thirties. We had to check the back lanes as well as the street. If kids were hanging around a corner and saw a cop coming they'd all walk away. You didn't have to speak to them. When you passed maybe they'd come back but you passed the point and that was it.

Then I went on Traffic and worked at Bridge and Wellington for two years. I was the last traffic cop at that spot because then they put the lights in. When I left Traffic I went to the Mounted Division. They were my best years. I enjoyed patrolling Mount Royal and I enjoyed riding a horse. They were paying me to do what I loved to do. (laughs) Did you ever ride a horse up on the mountain? Beautiful. Saddle up and go up there for eight o'clock, have your coffee at the chalet and ride down the pathways. We had no problems up there. A few kids lost and the odd drunk but nothing serious. There was one murder on the east side of the mountain. A kid was killed but I wasn't on duty when that happened. It was very cold in winter but it didn't bother me. I love the cold. It's the heat I can't stand. Once every three weeks you took your turn and went down to Bonsecours and did the traffic down there on horseback. And, of course, every time there was a riot or a strike you were on duty. There were a large number of horses then. We had forty-two but today they only have about twelve. We had standard-bred horses which were very gentle. Today they have Palominos and they are a nervous type of horse.

I worked for twelve years in Griffintown; five years as a sergeant, three years as a lieutenant and four years as acting captain. The case I remember most was the Fahy murder case in Point St. Charles. I knew the family very well. I knew the girls because I belonged to the Dramatic Club with them at St. Gabriel's Parish and, in fact, their mother and my mother worked together in the CNR as charwomen. The son killed his widowed mother and one of his sisters, hacked them up and threw them in the basement. I was the first policeman on the scene. By the time the detectives got there, the other two daughters had returned from work. They came crying to me and I got Doctor Duffy to come over and sedate them. I then went home and got into plain clothes and we found the boy who did it at four o'clock in the morning in Lachine. He died in the mental hospital. His mother had been advised to put him away but she wouldn't do it. There was an older brother but the two sisters remained in that house and lived there for years. They never married. It was a terrible, terrible story.

Normally, uniformed policemen weren't involved in solving murders. It was always the homicide people who took charge. Suicides were another matter. We had to stay there until the body was removed to the morgue and then we had to appear at the inquest. I must have investigated about 50-60 suicides over the years. I had to pull a few suicide bodies out of the Lachine Canal. Terrible. I remember one time there was a body that must have been in the canal for five or six months. The two cops who were there before I arrived jumped in their car and got away. The morgue officials told me to take the body out. I said, "No, you take it out." He said, "No, we don't take it out. The police take it out." So I had to reach down and pull the body up. I was sick for about a week. I was going to suspend the two cops who left the scene but they said, "We couldn't do it. We're married and have kids." I said, "Aw, forget about it." The worst of it was after I got my reports made the inspector called me and told me to go back to the morgue because I hadn't searched the man's pockets. So I had to go back but the guy at the morgue said that he would do it. You never get used to that kind of thing, you know. There were a lot of suicides in the thirties.

Jean Drapeau started the Bloc Populaire Movement in the forties. Some of their rallies would end in riots and we were down there morning, noon and night. There were some very severe riots and we had a lot of policeman injured.

There was also another huge demonstration around Delormier Street of welfare people. They wanted work and they wanted food. We didn't have too much food either, even as policmen. It didn't feel too good to put down riots like that. I was stationed at No. I and there were maybe, 300-400 policemen called out for that one. The inspector told us to turn our badges so that nobody could read our numbers. You get so mixed up in a riot. You're in amongst a group and trying to protect yourself. I remember an old lady fell down and I went to pick her up. The inspector grabbed me and said, "Don't pick anybody up. Keep moving." It was odd but that's the way things were. There were a lot of strikes at that time too; the stevedores' strike and the textile strike in St. Henry. We were there for months and a lot of policemen were injured. They'd be up on the roof throwing rocks at us. (laughs) It wasn't an easy life, that's for sure.

I also remember the disaster in Griffintown. Oh, my God. Was it ever terrible. The whole Polish crew was killed when the bomber went down. I had just talked with "Jolly" Lemieux, the traffic cop, before I went to the station. When the accident happened, I rushed back and was the first policeman on the scene. I was in charge for maybe half an hour before senior officers came down and took over. It was all over by the time I got there. We were just trying to keep the people from infiltrating the area where the plane was but Lemieux was killed in that crash. He went down to visit a friend and we found his gun and badge amongst the rubble. That was a terrible, terrible tragedy.

Another terrible tragedy was the Bonaventure Station fire which occurred in the forties after the war. The fire broke out in the evening. I was a sergeant then and I had ten or twelve men with me to control the huge crowd. The inspector came down and said, "I'm bringing in the Mounted Division." I said, "Please, Inspector, don't bring them down here. Horses are good for crowd control but they're not used to fires." He said, "They're on their way here now." I think there were six mounted policemen who came down. There were drums in the back of the station and when they started to explode the horses took off. There was a rumour that one of the horses was found down around Pie IX Boulevard. I don't know if he still had a rider or not. (laughs)

During World War II they were looking for police officers to go into the Provost Corps when the First Division was formed and four or five of us signed up. We were going to be Regimental Sergeant Majors, whatever that meant, but after we signed up we were taken downtown and told that we couldn't go, that we had to stay in Montreal. They brought many Europeans over here to train and we had more riots here in Montreal than they had over in the war.

(laughs) These men would come in at Place Bonaventure or Windsor Station and go into all the bars on Peel Street where they would fight and vandalize the bars. Most were Czechoslovakian or Polish. The Americans also had a huge camp around Plattsburgh and thousands of men would come to Montreal on a Friday night. They were instrumental in closing all the brothels. The American government was having so much trouble with venereal disease that they caused the Montreal area to be tightened up. We used to get calls from hotels where there'd be 60-70 American soldiers half drunk and they couldn't be controlled. They'd fight with anybody at all if they were intoxicated. The Americans brought their own Provost people up and they used to stay at our station with us. When we got a call they'd come out with us and they'd handle their own people.

Montreal used to be a wide open city. Once I got a call from Paddy Lawton who was inspector of the West Division. He wanted me to work on the Morality squad. I said, "No, I won't work Morality." He said, "Why? Are you sick?" I said, "No, I'm not sick. I have enough trouble saving my soul without going on Morality." A cop on Morality in those days could make himself five or six hundred dollars a week by taking bribes. I wouldn't go on morality and I stayed in uniform. When the Langlois Probe was started to investigate policemen taking kickbacks, a lot of policemen, Irish guys included, had to pay a lot of money for legal fees in order to stay out of jail.

Once I was injured at a fire. The floor went down and I went down with it. (laughs) The worst injury I suffered was when I was sent down to control the crowd at a baseball game. This kid swung the bat and let it go just as I turned around. I was hit over the eye and was hospitalized for about four or five months. I very nearly went under that time. My nose and jaw were broken. We also used to have to settle fights in the Point. There used to be a very tough bar on Bridge and Wellington but we never had that much trouble. We'd go in and settle the fight and get out. I was never injured doing that.

The only thing that bothered me about being a policeman was too much free booze. (laughs) If you're a policmen on the beat everybody wants to give you a drink. I could start at St. James Street and walk up Peel Street and be loaded before I got to Dorchester if I took every drink that was offered me. There used to be about 15-20 clubs in those days on Peel Street.

I was only forty-nine when I took my pension. I had to do it because my pension from the Police Department was not very good. I could have spent another thirteen years there but when I was offered a job as chief inspector for the SPCA, I took it. The money they offered me was better than what I was making on the police force. They also gave me a car and I travelled all over Quebec. While I was working for the SPCA I met a senator from New York who introduced me to the president of the Windsor Hotel who hired me as chief of security. When he left the Windsor Hotel to go to work for Quebec Air I went with him. That's where I had the best time of my life because I travelled. I went to Rome. I went to Paris. I went to Hawaii. I also had three men working for me.

I used to be an executive member of the United Irish Societies. I censored the parade for several years. Anybody who was drunk, I had to throw them out. I made a few enemies because a guy who had been thrown out wouldn't talk to me for the rest of his life. I didn't mind them drinking as long as they could walk. (laughs) Did they eventually forgive me? Oh, yes, on their deathbeds.(laughs) In those days, the United Irish Societies had representatives from the Holy Name Societies of every parish and they formed the executive. Today they don't have any representation from the local parishes and I haven't been associated with them for years. John Loye was their historian and I was very much against it the day that they voted him out. He had been president for about twenty years and they should have left him there until he died. It was a group from St. Ann's that put him out. They came en masse and they all voted him out. I think they didn't like the way he was doing things. We never saw him again at any of the meetings and when he passed away he left everything to St. Patrick's Society. I think he was very bitter about that. He was a great historian in his day.

I'm sorry now that I didn't go into the elevator trade with the rest of my brothers. Becoming a policeman means that I have no security now. I only get a limited pension and my brothers all had good pensions. When indexation came in 1972 the policemen were able to retire with $20,000-$25,000 a year. I get $4,000 a year. One time we got together and got a lawyer who tried to fight our case but we didn't get anywhere. We tried to get them to give us the same amount of money they would give a man on welfare. They get $6,000 a year and we wanted them to give us the same amount. When I see a young policeman today I think how lucky he is to be making 40-50 thousand a year. (laughs) The policemen today don't have to do the hours we did but they have other problems. We never had drugs and taverns were not as active as they are today. They were places where men met and had a beer and that was it. If a fight broke out it was settled but today it carries on out to the street and there are knives and guns involved. We never had any of that. Never.

One of my sisters was murdered here in LaSalle a few years ago. Her name was Mary Mole and she was seventy-four years of age when it happened. She was hit on the head just down the street from where I live. She had had dinner with me on Thanksgiving Day and I said, "I have a hide-a-bed. Stay here." She said, "No, Jack. I'm going to go home." "Well," I said, "I'll get you a taxi." "No, No," she said, "It's a nice evening." She only lived a few blocks away in Verdun where she was active with St. Thomas More Parish. The two guys who did it were arrested but they didn't serve too much time in jail. One was a juvenile and the other one was of age. He was sentenced to two years less a day and he only served one-third of that. The motive was robbery but my sister didn't have any money on her. All she had was a car ticket in her hand. That broke us all up. My brother, who passed away a few years ago, wanted to kill the two guys but I told him to leave it to the police and the justice system.

John "Jack" Moore on mounted patrol on Mount Royal in 1939.
"They were paying me to do what I loved to do."
Courtesy of John Moore.

Hannah Moriarty

Hannah Moriarty was a very popular and talented entertainer in Griffintown. A dancer, singer and actress, she helped to create the memorable concerts put on by the St. Ann's Young Men's Society. Hannah was much in demand as a singer in the Irish community for over forty years. She recalls how her mother managed to get a piano for the family which made their home a popular meeting place for the neighbours in the days when most entertainment was home-made.

I was born on Ottawa Street in St. Ann's Parish. My parents were from Ireland but they both came here as young adults and were married in Montreal. They talked a lot about their families and told us how happy they were as children in Ireland. My father's favourite expression was, "Thanks be to God for our daily bread." My parents were very religious people who never missed Mass and we never dared miss Mass either. My father was a singer and my mother was a dancer so I was brought up with music. I was the eighth of nine children. My father worked at Montreal Light, Heat and Power which was just one block away from where we lived so he used to come home for lunch every day. We didn't have much money but, oh, the fun we had! I remember once my father wanted my mother to buy a fur coat for herself. She said to him, "What do I want a fur coat for just to go and get the meat every day?" He insisted and told her that he would take the day off to go and help her pick out a coat. My mother didn't want him to take the day off because he wouldn't get paid if he did. To make a long story short, he came home one day and said, "Did you get the coat?" She said, "Yes, it's in the living room." He walked into the living room and there was a piano. "That's my fur coat," she said. "Now don't say a word. We'll get more out of that piano than I would every get out of a fur coat." My mother was right. There was always something going on in our house. People would visit and sing songs. My mother would serve ginger ale, not big glasses, small glasses. After all, they didn't have that kind of money but she always managed to have something for the people who came and they usually came every night. My mother never served liquor but everybody got a small glass of ginger ale and a biscuit. Not many people had a piano in those days so if you had one, your friends would say, "Let's go to the Moriarty's." It was a wonderful time and I wouldn't trade it for anything.

I never took piano lessons. I just picked it up. I went to St. Ann's Girls' School and the nuns were terrific. They were the ones who taught us to sing in the concerts. And I was in many. If you played in one and they thought you were fairly good, you just kept on playing in them. Most of the shows were in St. Ann's Hall but once a year we'd have a show at the Monument National. When we'd be rehearsing for a play in St. Ann's Hall, it was not unusual for one of the priests to come over and sit on the side and just listen. They all liked the plays so much. I sang from the time I could talk, I guess. I started to entertain in public when I was about ten years old and I did it practically all my life, even after I was married. You had to study if you were in the plays. You didn't go there not knowing your lines or you were told off. They didn't fool around, not at all. I was usually the leading lady, not when I first started because then I was quite young but later on when I got more experience. I remember Jimmy More, from St. Anthony's was often my leading man in the concerts. When I started out, my mother said, "You come right home after the show. Don't let anybody take you home." I never did let anyone take me home because she would have stopped it. You went to sing, you sang and went home. Leo Bracken used to direct many of the plays. The Brackens were good parish helpers. Whatever the parish wanted to do, they'd help and they didn't get paid for it, of course.

On St. Patrick's Day I usually stayed home. That meant that I missed the parade but once you've seen one..... I stayed home and stayed quiet because I wanted to save myself for the evening. I didn't go out or run around or anything like that. The Monument National was a beautiful theatre and the place used to be jammed. You couldn't get a seat. People came from all over the city. There would be a play with three acts and in between acts they would have a singer or a dancer. It started at eight and usually ended at eleven. After the play a gang of us used to go to Mother Martin's Restaurant and have a drink and sing songs while somebody played the piano.

My brother Jack was a bridge player and, at one time, he was the best player in Montreal. They used to send him to Quebec and Toronto to play. My sister Margaret became a schoolteacher and Kathleen used to dance in the concerts. My brother Pat directed some of the plays. Everyone in our family was involved in something. We all stayed in Montreal and remained close to one another. The Depression did not affect my family, thank God. My brothers Jack, Pat and Bill worked for the CPR and two others worked for Montreal Light, Heat and Power so they were all in fairly large companies. I worked in the Accounting Department of the Bell and you didn't lose your job unless you wanted to lose it, if you know what I mean.

I left Griffintown when I got married. I met my first husband when I sang for Police Inspector Lawton who was his father. We moved to N.D.G but it wasn't the same as being in a big family where there was always something going on. I worked for the Bell all my life. I had a good job, which I loved, and the Bell was a wonderful place. I sang in concerts at night but I never sang in the daytime.

What influenced me most in life was my home, really and truly. My mother had a wonderful attitude. If you were bringing somebody home for dinner, she wouldn't go out and get something extra. If the food was good enough for her family, it was good enough for anybody who came in so you never had to warn her in advance. What she served you was good enough for anybody you were bringing home which was a wonderful way to be.

In the concerts, I used to sing mostly Irish songs that people knew. Did you ever hear, "The Englishmen They Own St. George's Street?" I'll sing it for you.

> Oh, the Englishmen they own St. George's Street
> The Welsh, they have St. David's Lane
> Now the Jews are very fond of Craig Street
> Every nation owns the Main.
> The Scots, they live on Argyle Avenue
> And the French, they stay in Côte St. Paul
> But the Irish you can't beat
> For they own St. Patrick's Street
> Every nation has a street in Montreal.

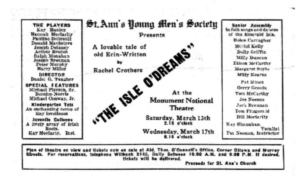

A postcard advertising the 1937 production of the
"Isle O'Dreams." Hannah Moriarty's name can be seen
at the top left corner.
Courtesy of the Burns family.

John Patience

John Patience was born in Belfast on August 30, 1918. Canada's post-war boom led many companies to recruit young, educated people from overseas and John was part of this particular migration. He arrived in Montreal in 1953 with his wife, Isabel, and two small children. As a member and past-president of the Irish Protestant Benevolent Society, John has played an active part in the Irish Protestant community of Montreal. He joined the Masonic Order in Belfast in 1940 and soon after his arrival here, joined The Lodge of Antiquity.

The earliest memory I have of Belfast is when I was about four years of age. There was a lot of trouble in the city and people were rioting. The Irish Free State was going independent at that time and I remember my uncle coming home all covered with muck. He had been out after curfew and a police car (maybe the Black and Tans) had come around the corner unexpectedly and he dived into a hedge. (laughs) That's the earliest memory I have of my childhood—seeing my uncle covered in muck standing in the kitchen while everybody had a good laugh.

We lived in the area called Ballymacarret which is predominantly a Protestant area so consequently there was no friction at all. I remember the time when I went with my group of Wolf Cubs to see the Parliament Building (the Northern Ireland Parliament Building at Stormont) when it first opened. It was a beautiful building, absolutely beautiful, and I remember looking at the statue of Carson[*] outside the building. We were part of a large contingent of youngsters from youth organizations who were called out for the occasion of the opening of the Parliament Building. I also remember Carson's funeral. We all got out of school that day to go and line the streets and add to the numerical quantity of the people who came to mourn Carson.

I had the misfortune to lose my grandfather and uncle (my father's youngest brother) in the Blitz during World War II. I believe it happened on the fifth of May in 1941. I was in the Home Guard at the time and, as soon as the siren went, it was my job to put on my tin hat, put my rifle on my back and get up into the Castlereigh Hills just in case there were any downed German airmen to be picked up. So that's where I watched the Blitz that night but when I got back down to the city the next day I found out what had happened to my grandfather and my uncle. That was a sad time for us. I think the city of Belfast lost more than one thousand people on that particular night. My parents lost their home in another raid when an unexploded bomb dropped on a house a few doors from us. The people got cleared out and the bomb went off the next morning and wrecked a few houses. We then had to find new accommodation which wasn't too difficult because most people were getting out of the city. We had three air raids on Belfast and two of them were pretty severe.

My father was an Orangeman so we celebrated the 12th of July. (laughs) We would be up pretty early in the morning because you could hear the bands playing, pipes and all, and we would go and see the Orange Lodges assembling at Ballymacarrett Orange Hall which was a couple of hundred yards from where we lived. We'd watch them head off to the marshalling point in the centre of the town and then we'd take off and go up the Lisburn Road where we'd stand and watch the various lodges going by. It took a long time, three and a half or four hours. One year I was in the parade. I guess I must have been of an entrepreneurial nature because I found that you could get sixpence for carrying a musician's case. I carried the case of a clarinetist and I walked about four miles to the marshalling point (which was called The Field) and four miles back, all for sixpence.

Growing up, we stayed more or less in our own neighbourhood. We played soccer against Catholic groups and I used to play water polo and swim against Catholic swimming clubs but then we went our separate ways again. Of course, we went to separate schools. You see, that's the great tragedy of Northern Ireland. Once you're six years of age you're streamed into the Protestant system or the Catholic system and you really don't get to make many friends from the other group.

After my elementary education I studied electrical engineering at the College of Technology. Later I took the Higher National Certificate in electrical engineering. I was an apprentice draughtsman in the shipyard of Harland and Wolff and was going to the College of Technology three nights a week for about six years. Seems a long time, doesn't it? I eventually branched off and became a marine engineer. Canada always got its naval ships from Britain and the few that were built in Canada were built to British design so the Government of Canada decided it was time to form an organization which would design and build ships here and I was recruited in the U.K. to come and be part of the organization. I came to Montreal first class Cunard, not steerage, because the company was paying. (laughs) I started to work at Canadian Vickers. I came on April 15, 1953 and started work right away. I stayed with the company until 1983 when I retired. When I came to Canada, I was thirty-four years old and Belle and I had a girl of six and a boy of two.

John Patience, shown here wearing the President's Chain of Office
of the Irish Protestant Benevolent Society. Born in Belfast, John
was part of the post-war migration of educated workers
which helped fuel Montreal's growth in the fifties.
Courtesy of John Patience.

The tough part is leaving family behind. I realize how it must have saddened my parents because I would hate anyone to take my three grandchildren away from me. I tried to get back for a visit as quickly as I could but in those days five dollars was a lot of money and a couple of thousand pounds to take the family back to Northern Ireland was out of the question. Eventually we did get back after nine years and spent a month over there. From that point on we tried to return every couple of years to give the grandparents a chance to see how the children had grown.

A friend who worked at Vickers put us up for a few days until I managed to find a duplex. We lived on Viau Street between St. Zotique and Beaubien. Was it in the heart of French Montreal? It wasn't in the heart of anything in those days because my nearest neighbour was a brown cow! (laughs) The city hadn't extended that far then. There was a pond and fields where the children used to play. There was an English school on Beaubien Street and a Presbyterian church on Rosemount Boulevard which wasn't too far away. They referred to that area as New Rosemount.

We rented a brand-new duplex and stayed there for fourteen years. Many of the people I worked with were from Belfast and Glasgow (Belfast and Glasgow being two big shipbuilding centres) and we more or less stuck together. We had parties together, played golf together, stuff like that. We really didn't integrate into the Irish milieu which was largely Roman Catholic. Neither did we integrate into the French milieu although I spoke French, having learned it at school. Eventually, these friends moved away and took their jobs with them.

We left Rosemount and moved to Ville D'Anjou in 1967. I liked Ville D'Anjou and I got on very well with my neighbours. It's a nice little town and at that time it was half French and half English. Remember, there was a large segment of the English-speaking population of Montreal who worked in the east end at the oil refineries, Canadian Vickers, Canada Steel Wheel and Montreal Locomotive. Most of their technicians and engineers were English speaking and Ville D'Anjou was a nice convenient place to live. When my children branched out on their own, they worked either downtown or in the western part of the city and one night my son said to me, "You know, Dad, you're retired and you don't have to live in the east end of the city. Why don't you come and live in the west end to be close to your grandchildren?" I felt that that was a good idea because I was getting rather tired of driving the Metropolitan twice a day, four days a week, simply to see the grandchildren so we moved to the West Island in 1988.

Do I regret coming to Canada? I'm not unhappy that I came but I sometimes wonder if I would have fared any better if I hadn't come. Of course, it's not ponderable, is it? You can't really answer that one but certainly, at the time that I decided to come to Montreal things were not awfully good in the United Kingdom. People will remember that we were still rationed after the war and the cost of living was very, very high. It was tough to make ends meet. By the time you paid your mortgage and your taxes, there wasn't too much money to throw around. The post-war boom came four or five years after I left.

My hope for Northern Ireland is what everybody hopes: that eventually there'll be peace in the place and it will get back to the prosperity that it once knew. I think it must be remembered, too, that's it's not one-half of the population against the other half. There's a small group of lunatics on either side and that's the only word I can use to describe them. They are a very small group and my hope for Northern Ireland is that somehow the population itself will get rid of them by giving them no support. If they were ostracized completely the country could get back on track. It's a great little place and it was a marvellous place in which to grow up. The education system is exceptionally good and there are a lot of very skilled and talented people over there. The last time I was there, I noticed a few cosmetic changes to the place. Certain slum areas have been knocked down and rebuilt and it looks quite attractive. When I'm there, I'm not anxious to get back to Montreal. I enjoy being there but when I get back here I say, "It's good to be home."

*Sir Edward Carson (later Lord Carson of Duncairn,) was born in 1854 in Dublin. A lawyer and politician, he was known as the uncrowned king of Ulster. Mistrusting Irish nationalism, he became the leader of northern Irish resistance to Home Rule and in July of 1914, agreed to Home Rule for Ireland apart from Ulster which was effected in 1921. He died in England in 1935 after many years of service to the British government.

Margaret Eason Davidson

Margaret Davidson's early years were spent in the rarefied atmosphere of Montreal's Golden Square Mile. Her father was employed as a chauffeur to the A.D. MacTier family and Margaret and her family lived in the coach house. A.D. MacTier was born in Scotland in 1867 and came to Canada in 1887. He had a long and successful career with the Canadian Pacific Railway; working his way up from stenographer to his appointment in 1918 as vice-president, Eastern Lines. He died in 1940.

I was born on October 30, 1919 on Dominion Street in St. Henry. My mom came from Drumein in County Louth and my dad was born in Brighton, England. His parents were of Irish heritage, I believe. When my mother was young she worked as a maid in one of the biggest hotels in London and then she and a friend saved their money and came to Canada. She worked for the Andrew Allan family as a lady's maid and she met my father in Cacouna which is near Murray Bay. She got married late in life—she was about thirty-one which was considered late in life in those days. My mother was six years older than my dad. They had one little girl, Mary, who died when she was about three-and-a-half and I was the next child. I must have been around two when Mary died. Then there's Rita, my sister who died of cancer in 1968, then Jimmy and Kathleen.

Mother had lived such a funny life in Ireland. Her home life was very narrow-minded. Most of the boys she went out with served on the altar and she said that when they would come home with her on a Sunday after church they weren't allowed in the house. She always said that when she had children she would allow them to have their friends in. She couldn't stand de Valera and that's all we ever heard when we were kids. She used to say that he was a terrible, terrible person. She liked Lloyd George of England. Her whole family was loyal to Britain because they all worked for the government. They ran a Post Office which was attached to their house. She had seven brothers and most of them were in the police or the military. There was one brother who was beaten and left to die by the side of the road. The nationalists must have considered him a traitor. They found him and brought him home but he never worked after that and I think he died a few years later. My mother could never forgive them for that. One of her other brothers had his house and all his new furniture burned down on his wedding day.

My father was sports-minded and a very good boxer. He held the lightweight championship and the welterweight championship of Montreal way back in the twenties. His name was Batholomew Eason. He had about five brothers but only one of them came to Canada. We moved from Dominion Street in 1923. Daddy worked as a private chauffeur for the vice-president of the CPR, A.D. MacTier and we lived in the coach house where the Westin Mont-Royal Hotel is now, on the corner of Sherbrooke and Peel. We lived there for many years, right up until around August of 1942. We were brought up in the Golden Mile area and most of the children we played with all had parents who worked for these very well-to-do people like Lady Drummond, Lord Shaughnessy, Lady Allan, Sir Herbert Holt, Sir Mortimer Davis and the Refords from the shipping company. We weren't brushing shoulders with them but they were all in our life. The people in the Golden Square Mile were not like the nouveau riche. They were born into money and they were friendly and nice but they kept their distance. I think we learned the value of nice things and how things were done. We saw how they dressed and we knew how they ate. The MacTiers were very good to us. They had a cook and a lady's maid and a table maid and a scullery maid. When the cook used to make gingerbread you'd smell it baking.

The coach house was lovely. We had two bedrooms, a very big living room, kitchen, bathroom and a long hall. Downstairs there was a cabinet that had beautiful old saddles and sleigh bells and they had a great big wine cellar. The floor of the garage was cement and there was a yard between the big house and ours and it was all cement which we didn't like very much because we wanted to pitch a tent and, of course, you couldn't pitch a tent in cement. We'd tie blankets and sheets to a window or something. The yard had a big gate where you could drive a car but we were never allowed to play on Peel Street or Sherbrooke Street. All the other kids were allowed to play out on the street but we had to play in our yard and, of course, we thought that was terrible. The yard was maybe four times the size of an average bedroom so you can imagine that we didn't have too much space to roller skate.

My mother had nothing to do with the big house at all. She just took care of the family and ran the house her own way. All my dad did was drive the car and he wore a uniform in those days, brass buttons and leggings, very formal. We drove around during the Depression in a Packard, I'd like you to know, and not an old Packard; every two years they got a new car. "Ask the man who owns one," that was the Packard motto.

Our door was never locked and when our friends came my mother would make sandwiches and buy us a bottle of Flirt which was five cents in those days. It was like purple water and came in a big, huge bottle. We'd play Truth and

Margaret Davidson's family circa 1927.
From left to right, Rita, Kathleen, her mother Kathleen Hynes,
Jimmy, Margaret, and her father Bert Eason who worked as a
chauffer for the A.D. MacTier family in Montreal's
Golden Square Mile.
Courtesy of M. Davidson.

Dare and Postman and Spin the Bottle. Between the kitchen door and the pantry door we made a little office and that was our post office. You'd take a shine to one boy and then you'd go around the room and you'd say, "I want to send so many stamps to such and such a place and I'll take Johnny," and you'd have to give him five kisses for five stamps. It was all very innocent. Sometimes we'd close all the blinds in the afternoon after school and we'd tell ghost stories. We'd see who could tell the scariest story.

Sometimes when the weather was nice in the summer my mother would pack a great big box with sandwiches and cucumbers and everything and my father would take us out to Jacques Cartier Beach or to some other little beach. We were so happy to go and my sister and I used to pray that it would rain because whenever we prayed for nice weather it always rained. My dad hated the picnics but he never said a word. He'd bring a soccer ball because he used to play for the Sons of England. If he could find some men at the beach, they'd have a game. If not, he'd sleep in the back of the car.

We had a very good, a very loving childhood. My dad was kind and good but extremely strict. Mother learned from being brought up in a narrow-minded and strict home to be loving and kind. Very often she'd go to Daddy and say, "You know, the girls want to have people in." My dad just adored my mother. She could do anything she wanted with him. All you had to do was ask Mother to ask Daddy and it was a fait accompli.

Mother came to Canada around 1911 or 1912 and she always wanted to go back to Ireland to see her family. We weren't rich and one day my dad came home and he said, "Kathleen, Mr. MacTier booked your passage, tourist class, on a CPR ship but I won't be able to go with you. You'll be going with the children." I was about five or six at the time and my sister Kay was only about nine months old. We must have landed in Ireland in the middle of April and we stayed until August. We went to school for a while in Ireland and I learned how to ask to go to the bathroom in Gaelic. I still remember how to say it. We went to school out under the trees. The church and the school yard were just across the road from the house. We sat on benches which was quite a novelty because Montreal didn't have anything like that.

My grandmother and grandfather, who were pretty old by this time, ran the Post Office with one of my mother's sisters. You went through a door from the rest of the house and the Post Office was there. It had all the things for the mail and the door was always locked and we, as children, weren't allowed to go in there and touch anything.

My grandmother found it quite strange that Rita did not like a lot of butter on her toast or anything like that but this little pig here; treacle, pancakes, give me the kitchen sink and I'd eat it so I was the apple of my grandmother's eye. I remember two of my uncles, Berty and Charlie. Charlie was very manly and very good looking but he wasn't as handsome as Berty. When they took us out riding on their bicycles I had to go with Charlie and I remember throwing pepper in his face because he wasn't as handsome as Berty. They had three goats and I remember going out in the evening to pick stinging nettles. We used to go out and feed the chickens and pick flowers and play with the old-fashioned ovens they had in the fields. Rita and I would go out in the morning and help the lady next door put the cows out and Mother was always afraid that we'd get hit by a cow's tail because cows have a wicked tail. One day Mother walked us to Dundalk. It was raining and Kathleen and my brother were in a little go-cart. Rita and I walked and Mother bought us boy's boots because we were out among the cow dung and everything and she wasn't going to buy us fancy little shoes like the ones we had in Montreal. Rita and I screamed and cried all the way back home. We were mortified. We were very proud children and we were always mortified. That's the way we were. Everything had to be just so. They wanted to keep me, little Sucky, in Ireland, and I was quite willing to stay but my mother didn't dare go back to Canada minus one child. My father was a very family-oriented man and that wouldn't have gone over very well.

I remember the boat trip there and back. We went on the *Metagama* and I never got seasick because I ate like a pig the whole time and they say the more you eat when you're on a boat the less sick you are. Mother nearly died. She was just getting over the birth of a baby nine months before and wasn't strong at all. There was a steward who used to come and help her by minding the baby so she could get a little sleep. Once I was supposed to be minding my brother who was about three years old and I dropped him on the second deck and he got a big egg on his head; I got a good spanking for that.

Mother always said that she enjoyed her trip and she was glad she went back but she'd never go again. You know the old saying, "You can never go back." She always said you couldn't go back. As children we could never understand what she meant. My mother wrote to my grandmother quite regularly. Her mother outlived her. They never told her when my mother died of cancer. Mother was fifty-seven when she died in 1942. Dad lived to be fifty-seven also and died of heart trouble in 1948.

My mother was Roman Catholic and my dad was Protestant. They were married in St. Patrick's Church and Daddy had to sign papers to bring the children up Catholic. My dad was a very good and honest man and when he said something he meant it and he never interfered with the way my mother brought us up. I went out with a boy and it was the same circumstances with the two religions and the father used to hide their clothes on Sunday so they couldn't go to church and carry on something terrible. My father knew his father from the Buffalo Lodge and we used to make comparisons between the two of them. I changed my religion when I was about twelve or thirteen to Anglican because there wasn't much going on in Quebec for Catholic girls at that time. I became a member of St. George's Church down on Windsor Street and joined the Girl Guides. My mother was a very beautiful lady, very straightforward. We begged and begged to change and she said, "I've done my duty. I've brought you up the way I was taught, the way I know how. If you're going to be Anglican and join the church, be Anglican and if you're not, then don't. You've reached the age of reason and now you're choosing what you want." All of us were married in the Anglican church. For the first six years I went to a Catholic School, Bourget Academy. It was half English and half French and then I went to a Protestant school.

Mother, however, didn't approve when Dad wanted to join the Masons in the thirties. She had a picture of the Sacred Heart in the kitchen with all our names on it. It was the Society of the Sacred Heart and Dad tried to get her to take it down when the Masons were coming because they come and interview you and you have to be voted in by people who see if you're fit to belong. It's like a golf club. I think he took it down but Mother put it right back up because nobody was going to tell her that because he was joining the Masons that she was going to take down her picture and if the Masons didn't like the Sacred Heart picture then that was going to be Daddy's tough luck but, anyway, Daddy got in the Masons!

During the Depression, luckily we were never on relief but my mother would often give a dollar or two to help her friends and acquaintances who were. We never went without a meal but sometimes we had to wait to get a new pair of shoes until the next payday or maybe Mommy couldn't buy two pairs of shoes on the same payday. I've put felt from an old hat in my shoes and I've put paper in my shoes and things like that but we never went hungry and we had a lot of love. We were taught never to tattle and I would no more tattle on my brother or sisters or they on me unless we did something terrible then we'd have to tell my mother but otherwise never. My father didn't like tattlers; the tattler got a smack as much as the person who did it because he didn't encourage squealing. We could have our little fights for two minutes to get the venom out of our systems and then after that it was civil behaviour. You had to talk civil to your brother and sisters at all times. We were brought up with kindness and understanding. We could go to our parents and talk to them.

Mr. MacTier died in 1940 and by then, of course, war was on but Dad was too old to go to war. He stayed on for a while as a private chauffeur for Mrs. MacTier. He adored her because she was a beautiful lady, very much like the old Queen Mother, stately and nice. The lady's maid acted more like the lady of the house than Mrs. MacTier did and I think she thought she was too; she had all the airs and graces.

In 1942 my parents moved to Dorion Street and my mother died shortly after they moved. By then I was married and had a family and my sister was married to a soldier overseas. He was killed at Caen in France. Jimmy and Kathleen were still young and were at home with my dad. My dad had two jobs; the last ten or fifteen years that he worked for MacTier, he had a night job at the Army and Navy Club near the Strand Theatre as the night manager. He had a beautiful singing voice and was the master of ceremonies. He was in vaudeville and he used to arrange concerts especially during the Depression to get food and things for different churches in Montreal. They'd have ten or twelve people, get a program made up and then give a concert and charge about fifty cents or a dollar and give the money to the churches. My dad was one of the first people to sing on CFCF/Marconi when they opened the station and we heard it on a crystal set. He had a beautiful tenor voice and he sang "Molly Malone."

I got married at twenty and had my two sons. One son is in Montreal and the other one is in Ottawa. Then I remarried in 1955. His name was Fred and he used to say to me, "You're always yelling and screaming like a mad Irishwoman." I always had a hot temper as a child. As I got older I realized that if I carried on the way I used to, screaming and yelling when the kids made me mad, I would end up with a heart attack. I wasn't hurting the kids. I was only hurting myself so when I was forty-two or forty-three I got some brains in my head and stopped all that silly nonsense. I was married to Fred for more than twenty years and then he passed away.

Kay Peachey

Kay Peachey was born on Christmas Day in 1921. An only child, she grew up on Young Street in Griffintown until the family moved to Notre Dame Street. Although her second home was part of St. Patrick's Parish, she continued to attend services at her beloved St. Ann's. The next move was to Verdun where she lived until her death in 2000.

My maternal grandparents were born in Ireland. My mother's mother came from Cashel in Tipperary. She was a Dwyer and my grandfather was a Keating from Limerick. My father's father came from Yorkshire in England. My father's mother was a Daley who was born in St. Ann's parish. Her parents were from Ireland. I guess you could say that I'm three-quarters of Irish descent. Growing up I was aware of the troubles and I loved listening to the old rebel songs like "Kevin Barry" and "The Rising of the Moon" but there was no anti-English sentiment in my family because my grandfather was English. I don't think he had any bad feelings toward the Irish either. It was mutual respect.

We rented a house on Young Street from my aunt and uncle. My mother's sister was married to John Gallery who had a bakery—he was a lovely man. Before I was born they had moved up to McDougall Avenue in Outremont. He belonged to the Young Irishmen's Society and I used to ask my mother why they were called the Young Irishmen because they were all so old. His sister, Auntie Kate Gallery lived just up the street and any person who came to Canada from Ireland seemed to go to her house. She always had these immigrants staying with her for a while until they got on their feet and on New Year's Day Uncle John would bring them around to visit everybody. This was a ritual, you know.

My dad was fortunate because during the Depression he was one of the ones who was working all the time. He worked for the CNR as a policeman. He was in the Investigation Department and they controlled the traffic on the Victoria Bridge. The company asked him if he would be willing to take nights. He did and for seven years he did night work all the time. He was glad to take it because he thought if he didn't they were looking for excuses to lay people off. What I remember the most would be sometimes he'd come home with his paycheque and there'd be a notice in it that effective next pay there would be a decrease in salary. This didn't just happen once. It would happen frequently and it affected everything in your life. My father accepted it because he saw so many who either weren't working or who worked for the Corporation in snow removal or street cleaning. Working for the City meant that you would get only a couple of

Kay Peachey photographed outside St. Ann's Church, January 1, 1943.
"Most of the young men were ready to go to war in 1939. Don't
forget it was at the end of the Depression. There wasn't any work
and it was a chance you took."
Courtesy of Kay Peachey.

days work because the foreman would try to share the work to give everybody a few days but yet it wasn't really enough for them to live on. You were always aware of the Depression and my mother would say, "We won't be able to do this," or, "You won't be able to get that." Some families were on relief and there were soup kitchens too but usually the people who went to them were single men, not fathers of families.

I think the people in Griffintown were really compassionate because I remember as a youngster going into the grocery store—my mother had an account at Paddy Murphy's—and I remember going to get five pounds of sugar and they had wooden floors and for some unknown reason I dropped the sugar and of course it went all over the floor. I started to cry because I thought my mother was going to be annoyed because I had wasted the sugar. Paddy Murphy said, "Now, now, don't worry about it." He told his wife to give me another bag and she said, "That's another five pounds." He said, "Oh, no. Only *one* bag on the bill." I always thought that was so kind. Mr. Murphy also sold beer and some people would take it to the yard behind the store. My mother used to call it Murphy's Beer Garden. Sometimes she would say: "The Beer Garden is busy tonight."

Some people looked down on Griffintown because of the number of taverns and blind pigs. I remember my mother saying one time that one of my cousins was visiting with her parents at someone's house and in the middle of the conversation she said, "When are you going to show me your blind pig?" You can imagine how fast they left.

Springtime was really a fun time because whether you were a boy or a girl you got out your marbles and alleys and the boys would really be mad if you ever so much as beat them at it. My mother wasn't too pleased because I'd wear the knees out of my stockings. You always waited for the warm weather to come so you could skip and play marbles. Marbles and alleys, I was always fascinated with them. I had roller skates as well. The parks didn't have things for climbing like monkey bars as they have today so we used to play in a yard that had all this stuff for the Corporation. We used to climb all over the rigs and all that kind of stuff. We would sit on top of this dump cart and let on we were driving for miles and there wasn't even a horse on it. I used to love it when the men would bring the horses and rigs home from the day's shift. When I was very little they'd sit me on the horse and let me ride into the stable and I thought that was really wonderful. Children are still children today. They're doing the same things that we did with our makeshift things.

The summers were always wonderful in Griffintown. Everyone used to follow the iceman when he came and pick up little chips of ice. The firemen used to put the hose on us to cool us off every night. We'd be in our bathing suits and some of us would have running shoes on. They would make the water go really high and down again, sort of make snakes with it. That was always a joy.

Sometimes we would go on picnics to Dominion Park. We used to love to go there. The parish would have a picnic somewhere and we would go to that too. Anyone with a car was somebody important and everyone who had a car seemed to share it. I remember there was one family with two sons and one of them became a fireman. I don't know how old he was but he must have been eighteen to be in the Fire Department. He would take the kids two and three at a time for a drive around the neighbourhood. You don't often find that today that a young man would be bothered with little kids.

There were a few cars on my street. The Greens had a Ford, a Tin Lizzie. He put up a garage in the yard made of corrugated metal and he used to take it out only on state occasions. I also remember the McCaffreys had a car and they used to take me out to St. Rose and Laval-sur-le-Lac. We thought we were going far, you know. Then Kinsella got a car so there were three cars on the street so I guess our street was more or less privileged. My uncle had the horses and rigs for the bakery and then he bought two trucks so it was horses and rigs and trucks and cars. My cousin had a car and so did my godfather and he would come and take us out.

Not everyone had a telephone so those who did shared. I remember someone was always coming to my mother to ask if they could use the phone. There was one family and their father often worked late. They would phone him to find out if he was working late that night because he didn't like to phone to give us a message. He was a very proud man so the daughter would come down to phone him at work. Everybody was like that. Whatever they had, they shared and you never felt that you were better than they were because you had a phone and they didn't. They must have felt at home to be able to share like that.

The Corpus Christi Procession would always be held on the Sunday closest to the day. Most of the people would paint their steps or put new oilcloth on their stairs. Sometimes they would paint their doors. My aunt always made sure that the painter came to paint the shutters before the procession. The whole parish would be in it. The First Communion children would be in their First Communion outfits and they would carry flowers and then there would be the altar boys, the sanctuary boys and the priests. Others participating would be the

Preparing for the St. Patrick's Parade on March 19, 1944.
Rev. Francis Kearney is dressed in the uniform of a military
chaplain. Beside him, wearing a top hat, is Percy Mullins.
Photo by Kay Peachey.

pupils from the boys' and girls' schools and the kindergarten. We would also have the Children of Mary and the Young Men's Society. The procession would come along William and down Young Street and stop at the No. 3 Fire Station which was on the corner of Ottawa and Young. Every year the firemen built this big repository and we would have Benediction there. If you ever pass down Ottawa Street and Young, you can look in and there's sort of an alcove between the station and the house beside it. The procession would all fit in around the station for Benediction. After that they would go to Basin Park, I think, and then into the church.

We also had bazaars and they were a great thing. They lasted for a week in the fall, usually early October, and were held in St. Ann's Young Men's Hall. You got an afternoon off school to go. They would have all kinds of booths and it was open every night from seven o'clock. I was so thrilled when I was finally allowed to go in the evening.

When Father Fee was at St. Ann's they had a bingo every Friday night. He would come to the school for catechism and if you answered his questions correctly he'd give you a free ticket to the bingo so then of course you brought your parents so it was good PR on his part. Later on the Sodality started having card parties, plays and bingos to help the church. We also had sleigh rides and after we'd come back to the church for beans and brown bread. Anything to help the parish.

I joined the Sodality and used to attend courses in Catholic leadership. We had at that time a union of parish Sodalities in Montreal so you would have to go and talk and express your ideas before others in the city and I think that probably gave us a good grounding in belonging to things and participating. We learned that if you want to do something, well you just had to get out and do it and not sit back and wait for someone else to do it. Your destiny is in your hands. You can't wait for someone else to shape it for you. We also learned to co-operate with others and this has continued in my life today because I'm quite active in the Catholic Women's League.

When I was a teenager I used to like to hike with my friends. I remember we would go hiking out across the river and go across the Victoria Bridge. We even walked across the Mercier Bridge. And we used to like to go sleighing and tobogganing. We would take our toboggans where Central Station is now. There was a big hole dug there and the CN didn't have the money to build Central Station during the Depression so consequently the hole was left and we would bring our toboggans up there and slide down in the wintertime. We would also go up to the mountain and Beaver Lake. We used to just go up there and hike around, go to the Chalet, things like that.

I think most of the young men were ready to go to war in 1939 because, don't forget, you were just at the end of the Depression. There wasn't any work and it was a chance you took. They knew that their families would be looked after and that the money would come home even if they went overseas. I remember one fellow who was in the army. I don't know if he went overseas but I know he worked at the Ordinance Depot on Notre Dame Street. He used to come home to visit his parents in the jeep and we thought this was the biggest thing in the world to see this jeep parked outside their house. We were all taken for a ride in it and we thought it was terrific.

Griffintown became so industrialized after the war that the people more or less had to move out. Most people who lived in Griffintown worked in the area so they had no cost for transportation like my father who worked at CN. That's why when they had to move they looked for something close like Verdun. When we came to Verdun we were the first people in this house which had just been built. I think anyone who moved from Griffintown at that period did so because of necessity. They had to move because companies were expanding.

I drive through Griffintown frequently. Every time I go uptown I always take the scenic route and go over Seigneurs Street Bridge because it's faster than going up Atwater. The kindergarten used to be where King's Transfer is today and although I never attended the kindergarten I feel sad when I see that the building is gone. Our school used to go there once a week and Major Long would have us march all around the hall. My house is still standing, but now it's an office supply company.

Tom Rowe

When Tom Rowe, of Islington, Ontario, heard about this project he was very anxious to share his memories of growing up in Griffintown. For many years after moving to Ontario he and his wife Rita maintained friendships with ex-Griffintowners and the first thing they did when they came to Montreal was to phone these old friends like Rita McCarthy whose late husband, Eddie Drouin, was one of Tom's best friends.

I was born on November 15, 1923 in Cardiff, Wales. Sometime thereafter my father emigrated to Canada and my mother and I remained behind. Although my father was highly educated and could speak several languages, my mother was not so fortunate; she had a very limited education and was employed mainly in domestic work. While we were awaiting his call to join him in Canada she worked as a housekeeper on the Isle of Man and I was sent to Liverpool to live with my grandmother, but happily I was able to spend the summers with Mother. I would be about three or four years old at the time.

Eventually the word (and money) arrived to have us join my father in Canada. This would be about 1929 or 1930 and after a tearful farewell to Grandma and Grandpa we sailed from Liverpool on the Cunard liner *S.S. Albertic* arriving in Halifax towards the end of November. I remember arriving in Montreal after a two-day train trip very vividly because it was the first time I had ever seen snow.

Daddy, as I called him, had a two-room flat on Notre Dame Street opposite what was then called the Grand Union Hotel. Shortly afterwards we moved to Basin Street and occupied a cold-water flat (they all were) which was directly below the Noonan family and opposite St. Ann's Church rectory. Our next door neighbour was a widow named Brannigan who had two children, Kathleen (nicknamed Cassie) and Nancy, who was about my age. Further down the street was a family named Forrester, with whom I became quite friendly.

Seven months after moving to Basin Street my father lost his job (as did many others) and we then began a series of moves which would take us out of Griffintown to St. Martin Street which was just west of Guy and then on to St. Antoine Street. This latter flat is etched in my memory because for the first time in my young life I encountered central heating. It was over a store at the corner of Guy and St. Antoine and we had hot water radiators.

Our joy was short-lived, however. The Depression was at its height in 1933 and although my father had some part-time work as an editor with a trade paper publishing house, he had to take on additional part-time work as a snow shoveller with the city. He had never done manual work before in his life.

After a hearty breakfast of sausages and eggs on a Sunday morning in March of 1933 my father complained of not feeling well, lay down on the bed and less than an hour later died of a massive heart attack. I was nine years old at the time. You can imagine my mother's dilemma. We were alone in a strange country, had few friends and no relatives of any kind. How was a widow with a nine year old son going to make ends meet? In any event, she decided to stay in Montreal rather than go back to Liverpool; the decisive factor being that she did not have the boat fare anyway and her intense pride did not permit her to ask her relatives in England for the money. I can still remember the doctor arriving at our house and pronouncing my father dead. He was flat on his back, eyes open, which the doctor closed and soon afterwards an ambulance arrived to take him away. Two days later he was buried in Mount Royal Cemetery, the reason being that he was an Anglican, as was my mother. Although he was born in very predominantly Catholic Wexford County in Southern Ireland and my mother was born on the Isle of Man, they were both Protestants.

My mother could not afford the flat we had on St. Antoine Street so we had to move. We learned from one of our Griffintown friends that a two-room flat was available on Olier Street and in May of 1933 we moved back to Griffintown. We were among friends again. In August 1940, full of patriotism, I joined the Canadian Army. I was sixteen at the time and lied convincingly that I was eighteen. I went overseas in February, 1941 and on my first leave went to see my grandparents in Liverpool. After serving throughout the Italian campaign our unit went on to Holland and in September, 1945 I was repatriated back to Canada along with the rest of the Canadian Army. During the war both my grandparents passed away.

If there is one memory that remains indelibly in mind to this day, it was the tremendous influence St. Ann's Church exercised in the minds of its mainly Irish congregation. It also extended to the less numerous parishioners of Italian and French descent. The nine o'clock Mass on Sunday was a mandatory event when the children of both the boys' and girls' schools would assemble by classes accompanied by their teachers, the brothers and nuns. The boys would occupy the centre left hand pews, the girls the right. The girls would be dressed in their school uniforms which consisted of white blouses and black skirts. The boys were expected to have clean shirts and well-pressed trousers and well-combed hair. Going to Communion was not only expected—it was required and anyone who did not do so had better have a valid excuse for not doing so. To say that you had inadvertently broken your fast by drinking a glass of water or something of the sort was unacceptable, the reasoning being that you had been paraded over to the church for Confession on the Friday preceding the Mass and you should still be in a state of grace and, if not, why not?

You may be wondering how an immigrant of the Protestant faith was assimilated into the Catholic religion. What happened was that when my father died and we moved back to Griffintown I was surrounded by my young friends, all of whom were Catholics, and I was permitted to go to St. Ann's School on Young Street. In due course, it was inevitable that I insisted on becoming a Catholic, to which my mother agreed. Soon after being baptized into the faith, I became a sanctuary boy and served Mass regularly, quite often during the early morning Masses during the week. There were two rewards for getting out of bed on a cold winter's morning at 5 a.m. to walk to church: the first being that you put yourself in line to serve Mass at a Saturday wedding, with a guaranteed nice tip, and the other was to be excused from going to school until 11 a.m. As I had to get up to throw a shovel full of coal on the fire anyway, it made a lot of sense to me.

In a nutshell, the Church, along with the schools, not only provided the discipline required during a period of deep Depression to keep the hope alive of better times ahead, but even more importantly it provided the glue that kept the congregation together. Although practically everyone was poor, you were constantly aware that there was always someone having a rougher time than yourself.

I spent close to seven years in St. Ann's Boys' School where the emphasis was on the three Rs. Each day starting at grade three we had a half-hour French lesson taught by a lay teacher, a French specialist brought in for the purpose. It was a no-nonsense school. Discipline was meted out with a leather strap across the hand. Depending on the nature of the offence, such as talking in class or being consistently late, the punishment was made to fit the crime. My own misdemeanours at times cost me anywhere from one to six strokes of the belt.

A typical day at St. Ann's started with a catechism lesson and then proceeded to the vital subjects such as spelling, correct grammar, composition, multiplication tables, fractions and in later years algebra was added. In grades nine and ten we were taught shorthand and typing and to this day I can still take, read and write Pitman's shorthand. This was an extremely practical approach because in the thirties a young man's dream of a first-class job was with the railway or some large company such as Bell Canada, or CIL, and they were extremely choosy in their hiring practices.

Usually, by the time grade ten was reached about half the boys had dropped out of school. By the time I made it to grade ten there were only a dozen of us left. Indeed, because I had put in some extra-curricular exercises in typing I too elected to drop out in March 1939 when I was offered a job at four dollars a week in the University Tower Building opposite Eaton's on University Street. The hours were 9 to 6:30 Monday to Friday, 9 to 1:30 on Saturdays. I walked to work each day. My duties consisted of taking shorthand, writing letters, sending out flyers, and any other gofer assignment that came up.

Homework was mandatory at St. Ann's but sometimes we had legitimate reasons for not doing it. For example, on one occasion when I lived on Olier Street in 1934 our electricity was cut off because of non-payment. For several weeks our only lighting was from coal oil lamps, and this during the height of the winter season. Heat was provided by a coal and wood burning stove with oven attached. For cooking we had a small gas stove but this was seldom needed in winter. Our greatest concern during the bitter winter weather was seeing that the wood stove did not go out during the night, which could lead to frozen pipes. Needless to say, there was no such thing as hot water plumbing. For that matter, in all the houses I lived in we did not even have a bath or a shower and I know the majority of homes in Griffintown likewise had no such conveniences.

By this time my mother had picked up a part-time job cleaning offices. Along with other Griffintown women they would make the trip by streetcar around 6 a.m., do their work, and get out of the offices before the staff arrived at 9 a.m. At other times she would perform similar chores at homes in Westmount. The pay: $1 to $1.50 per day plus carfare. The matrons in these houses would dispense two streetcar tickets. The cost of a streetcar ride was seven cents but a block of four tickets could be had for twenty-five cents. I guess these comparatively wealthy ladies also had cash flow problems.

How did the unwashed clean up? Simple, on Haymarket Square just off William and Nazareth Streets the City of Montreal operated a swimming pool plus bathhouse year round. Kids were admitted free but adults had to pay a nickel or dime. Boys could shower and swim for a half hour all year long on Mondays, Wednesdays and Fridays. Girls had Tuesdays and Thursdays, presumably because they were considered to be much cleaner than boys and not likely to get involved in such sweaty activities as baseball, soccer, football, and hockey. Saturdays and evenings were reserved for adults and on Sundays the bath was closed. Believe me, this facility was well used and it provided an essential service.

One of the highlights of the school year was participation in the annual St.

Patrick's Day Parade which took place on the nearest Sunday to March 17th, come rain, shine, snow, hell or high water. All I can remember of the several parades I marched in was that it was always bitterly cold, coupled with wet snow or heavy rain. So anxious was St. Ann's to make a top showing (there were apparently prizes for the parish with the best turnout) that the school hired a retired British Army sergeant major to teach us how to march properly. When I eventually joined the army I had no need for instructions in this part of army life and subsequently in October of 1945 when I was discharged from the army, I vowed that I would never be a part of any parade of any kind again. I have kept this vow religiously.

As Griffintown children reached the ages of eleven or twelve, we discovered a new source of enjoyment during the winter months apart from skating and hockey. It was Mount Royal and many a pleasant Saturday and Sunday afternoon was spent on its slopes. There were many routes to the mountain. You could walk directly up Peel Street to Pine Avenue and walk around the roads or take the stairway up to the Chalet and lookout. There were some four or five hundred wooden steps to the top. Alternately, you could take the streetcar up Côte des Neiges hill which was the west side, or take a streetcar to Fletcher's Field on the east side. We would take our toboggans, and as we got a little older, skis. I have even skied at night by the light of the cross. In those days no motor vehicles were allowed on the mountain but there was a streetcar available going from Mount Royal Avenue near Fletcher's Field that you could take to the area of the cross. Other than the streetcar, the only vehicles allowed were horse-drawn carriages and sleighs in winter.

In summer the Lachine Canal was used as our watering hole. Scores of boys used the canal as a swimming and diving facility and every once in a while the police would make a raid scaring the hell out of us for a day or so with threats of being thrown in jail the next time around. Two days later we would be back but at another location. One of the major attractions apart from lumber piles stacked along the basins were the Canada Steamship Lines ships and various train bridges which provided marvellous diving platforms. The crews of the ships wore themselves out trying to stop us from diving off their vessels.

In summer we had our baseball games. There was nothing more enjoyable on a hot summer afternoon than a game of baseball in Basin Street Park to work up a good sweat and then cooling off in the canal, sans bathing suits. Young girls would enjoy the spectacle, giggling and laughing, but with all due modesty, kept a respectable distance from the swimmers.

Entertainment in Griffintown was provided by plays staged at St. Ann's School with the most popular being the St. Patrick's Day Concert. Some of the songs I remember were: "I'll Take You Home Again Kathleen," "Come Back to Erin," "The Rose of Tralee," to name a few. As you can imagine, tears flowed freely at some of the sadder songs.

And then of course there was the Fairyland Theatre located at Inspector and Notre Dame Streets. For twelve cents you could see two full length movies, a serial such as The Perils of Pauline, or Clancy of the Mounted, which ran in twelve part segments for a dozen consecutive weeks, a comedy and Movietone News, in all a good four hours entertainment. Although you had to be sixteen to gain admission, nobody ever asked your age and on Saturday afternoon, for example, it was not uncommon for the place to be jammed with kids ranging in age from nine to thirteen. Needless to say, the main features on Saturdays were cowboy movies starring such luminaries as Tom Mix, Ken Maynard, Hopalong Cassidy, Hoot Gibson and other heroes of the time.

Probably though, the greatest entertainment, apart from the St. Ann's concerts, was provided by the radio. Frankly, the radio could only be described as a godsend. Not only did we get half-hour programs featuring such comedians as Jack Benny, Fred Allen, Fibber McGee and Molly, Bob Hope; there was also first class drama shows, soap operas and mystery shows galore, not to mention a goodly amount of musical performances. For all tastes, the radio provided everything anyone could desire, from the Metropolitan Opera to chamber music, to dance music and all the hits of the day. It was radio's greatest hour, in my view.

Griffintowners had their very own reason to be proud. On Saturday we were treated to a half-hour show put on by Moira Sheehy's Little Players of the Air, on CFCF. Although these kids were amateurs, they featured Irish tunes and dances and at least two or three of them were Griffintown natives.

Although we were in the height of the Depression, Griffintown boasted countless small stores, all of them specializing in soft drinks, candy bars, cigarettes and so on. There was literally a store on every corner and some located even in the middle of a block. Quite apart from the candy stores, there were countless grocery stores which stocked meat, fresh and canned vegetables and the big profit maker, beer, which sold for fifteen cents a quart, seven for one dollar. Turret and Sweet Caporal cigarettes were ten cents for a pack of ten, and you could get something called Zig Zag in an economy package at six for five cents. Then of course there was the "roll your own" package which was extremely popular.

A word about the stores would not be complete without some reference to Pesner's, located on Notre Dame Street. In the thirties, it was the forerunner of today's supermarket. Big, with contracts to supply ocean liners and lakers as well, it also operated a retail store. For many Griffintowners though, it had one serious flaw—it did not provide credit. All of the smaller stores did.

Also providing credit were the bread and milkmen. Serving Griffintown were four dairies, Borden's, Ernest Cousins, Elmhurst and Guaranteed Pure Milk. Bread and cake (the latter a luxury) were delivered by three or four bakeries, all on a daily basis. Horses and wagons were used in all cases and in winter before cars became numerous, it was not unusual to see the horses pulling sleighs instead of wagons.

Refrigeration during the hot summer months was supplied by a gentleman named Stacey. It consisted of a slab of ice which was carted into the house and dropped in the upper section of a wooden icebox. With any luck, it would last two days. To make sure it did so, my mother would have me wrap a newspaper around it.

Romance? By the time we had reached thirteen we realized that almost overnight, it seemed, the young girls whom we had teased so unmercifully were now developing into beautiful, graceful young ladies. Girls, too, seemed to agree that the boys they had looked upon with some contempt maybe weren't so bad after all, and perhaps had some redeeming features as they became more gentlemanly at long last. By the age of fifteen all of us were going steady and although we couldn't carry a girl's books home from school, we did meet on Friday nights in winter and carry her skates. In summer we might just go for a stroll on St. Catherine Street, usually with two or three other couples and get the girlfriend home in time for a little smooching in her porch, which was always broken up by a parent announcing, "It's time for your boyfriend to go home, so break it up."

If there is anything I remember about Griffintown more than anything else, it is the friendliness of the people of all walks of life. To the adults, a huge number of whom did not have jobs, it must have been heartbreaking not being able to provide more than the barest necessities of life to their offspring. Even more humiliating was the need on occasion to seek welfare and go on relief.

They did however, survive and even managed at Christmas to make certain that there was a gift of some sort under the tree. For its part, The Griffintown Boys' Club had a huge Christmas tree with donated gifts marked BOY or GIRL where the truly desperate could pick up a toy of some kind.

Forgive my nostalgia, but in looking back, I can only say that my memories of Griffintown are essentially the happy ones. The tough times, like my wartime experiences, would most certainly not want to be relived. Growing up in Griffintown during the Dirty Thirties is something I will always cherish—an eventful period I did not miss, and am grateful for it.

Tom Rowe carried this photo with him while he served overseas in World War II. This baseball game was played at Basin Street Park. The belfry of St. Ann's Church can be seen in the background, as well as Tom's home behind the swings. Ed Drouin is at bat and Emmett McGurk is the catcher. Among the players and spectators are such familiar Griffintown names as Frank Donnelly, Gerald Kelly, Maurice O'Connell, Joe Lynch, Teresa Boyle, Ray McLeod, Irene Normoyle, and Billy Burchell.
Courtesy of Tom Rowe.

May Cutler

May Cutler was born in Montreal in 1923 and grew up on Cartier Street near St. Joseph Boulevard. She holds Master's degrees from two universities, McGill and Columbia. During her varied career, she has been a journalist, professor, mayor, writer and publisher. In 1967 she became the founder and owner of Tundra Books, one of Canada's leading publishers of children's books. As mayor of Westmount from 1987 to 1991 she refused to go along with the renaming of the Westmount stretch of Dorchester Boulevard to Boulevard René Lévesque. Many English-speaking Montrealers admired the stand she took in what they saw as a campaign to slowly erase all evidence of the English presence in Montreal.

My maiden name was Ebbitt which, I presume, is a corruption of Abbott, a Scottish name probably going back to Cromwell's time. My father's name was William Henry and my mother was Frances Farrelly. My father was born in County Cavan—filthy County Cavan it was called by the Catholics of Ireland because it was a very Orange area. My mother was born in the next county, County Leitrim in the centre of Ireland. It's beautiful but it doesn't even have a hotel, so few people go there. Leitrim was half Catholic and half Protestant but Cavan was heavily Protestant. Both of these counties became part of the south of Ireland. They are on the border and of course a great deal of the trouble took place there, not too much in Cavan but a great deal in my mother's county. Her sister's husband was assassinated by the Sinn Feiners and so I grew up listening to all these horror stories.

Montreal, as I remember it from the thirties, did not have many Orangemen. My father went religiously to the Loyal Orange Lodge once a month and I went once or twice a year. I think the building was in Verdun. They had a parade on the Sunday closest to the 12th of July and marched on Peel Street. I remember seeing it once. My father wore his Orange sash. Very few Orangemen were in the parade, thirty or forty in the one that I remember and the parade sort of died out. I've always thought we were a minority within a minority but that's how the Irish probably felt in Quebec, too. I always felt close to the Irish Protestants of Dublin; so many of the great writers, Swift, Oscar Wilde and of course, Yeats.

My father said he came to Canada because he wanted to die as he was born— under the Union Jack. He just made it by a year or two. They changed the flag shortly after he died (laughs). I had two older brothers. My parents were in their thirties when they got married in St. Thomas Anglican Church in 1912. They bought two flats on Cartier Street. I think my mother's dowry was the down payment. My mother came from a very large family and she was sent out at the age of twenty-five, I think, to find a husband. She sailed into New York and stayed with relatives in different places in the United States. She didn't have any relatives in Montreal, but on the boat coming over to New York she met a Mrs. Ryan who owned a hotel on Windsor Street and became friendly with her. This is one interesting aspect on the cross movement between the Catholics and Protestants. Mrs. Ryan, who was Catholic, said, "Come to Montreal and you can stay with me." My mother came to Montreal. I don't know how long she stayed in the hotel, but then she decided to stay longer and took a job in a fruit store for a salary of two dollars a week. It was enough to support her in those days. Mrs. Ryan gave a party to which she invited the cop on the beat who was to become my father. Their parents knew each other vaguely. My mother used to say that they lived eighteen miles apart in Ireland but eighteen miles then was like 180 today.

My mother was a very outgoing person and talked to everybody. She was very dramatic. Hyperdramatic. A nut, really. I've often described it like having had Falstaff for a mother. She was a character and one of my friends used to do great mimics of her. My father didn't have many friends. He had two personalities: he hardly talked at home, or he sat and dreamed and recited very Victorian verse aloud. When he first came to Montreal he got a job in a box factory and then in 1909 he joined the Montreal Police Force where he stayed for twenty years. When he left in 1929 he became the doorman at the Royal Bank which had just opened on St. James Street. You had to leave the Police Force after twenty years or you couldn't collect your pension. He seems to have had an entirely different personality at work. People who knew him remembered him as good-natured and laughing. He was called Paddy and he was almost your classic Irishman. At home he was entirely different. My mother always seemed to be waking him from a dream or annoying his thoughts. He didn't pay much attention to his children except when he was roused by my mother over something my brothers had done. Brian Moore thought that this was common, the difference between the behaviour of the Irish outside the home and in the home. After about seven years at the bank my father retired and then spent most of the year at our country house at Lac Mercier.

I didn't get to school until I was seven because my mother overprotected me. She was in her forties when I was born and she was sure I was ill all the time. She used to wake me up with, "Are you well enough to go to school?" I remember one school incident. I must have had an Irish accent. I went up to the teacher and said, "I lost me scaaf." I remember her smiling and saying, "Repeat after me. I lost *my scarf*." I had problems with "ook" words like "book" and "hook" which my parents used, and I would always pause before I came to them so I would say them correctly.

I have to tell you this story. When I was four my parents moved to the second floor and we had tenants downstairs. We had a series of them and then the Labertés arrived with their eight children. My mother adored Mrs. Laliberté. She was one of those rare and perfect examples of the romanticised and ideal Quebec mother. She never raised her voice, she was always smiling and she worked from morning until night. Her husband was an electrician and they didn't have much money with so many children. She was always sewing and cooking and sending us up pickles. When Mrs. Laliberté came up the first of the month to pay the rent, my mother would take her into the parlour (which we never used) and offer her tea. In the living room was a table piano and above it, on the wall, a huge picture of King Billy crossing the Boyne; all in colour with a big gilt frame around it. My mother thought that it was offensive for a Catholic to have to sit in the parlour with King Billy on the wall so she started bringing Mrs. Laliberté into the kitchen for tea. Then the parlour got redecorated with an upright piano and there was no room for King Billy on the wall. The picture was moved into the dining room which was behind the parlour and dark in the daytime. Now my mother could invite Mrs. Laliberté back into the parlour. Mrs. Laliberté didn't speak English and my mother didn't speak French, but they seemed to understand each other. One day I came home (I was in high school and could speak a certain amount of French by this time) and found my mother and Mrs. Laliberté in the parlour. My mother said, "What is she asking me? Come and translate." Mrs. Laliberté wanted to know what had happened to that beautiful picture of Napoleon that my mother used to have on the wall! (laughs)

It's funny. My father had an almost abstract hatred of Catholics. He subscribed to *The Sentinel* which was full of stuff like the Vatican was taking over the world. Today it would be called a hate publication. But I know of no incident between him and Catholics. The ultimate example of this was when we bought a house at Lac Mercier (now Mont Tremblant). Next door to us were the Reynolds who were Irish Catholics. I think of them with sadness because one of their sons was killed in World War II. My mother was very friendly with Mrs. Reynolds and my father actually went fishing with Mr. Reynolds. Of course, they absolutely *never* talked about anything to do with religion or Ireland or politics. That was a

The Wearing of the Green—St. Patrick's Parade, 1988.
Westmount mayor (1987-1991) May Cutler atop a City of Westmount fire truck.
What would her father have thought?
Photo by Laureen Sweeney.

no-no. I thought this was a nice sort of situation to have arisen in Canada without carrying all this load with you. You wonder if the Serbs and Croats and the rest of them will ever see the light.

Our street was split between English and French and the English were split between Catholic and Protestant. The Catholic kids went to St. Dominic's and I didn't play much with them because they didn't get out of school until after four and we got out at 2:15. I went to DeLormier School on Gilford Street which is now an apartment building. I never saw any personal friction or fights between either the English and the French or the Catholics and Protestants. I went to Montreal High. I already knew that I wanted to be a journalist and I had scholarships right through high school. I also had scholarships at McGill. I was about the only person from my street who went to college. The English-speaking people on the street, which was working class, were immigrants from England and Scotland, not so much from Ireland. The Irish had come earlier. We always thought that the Catholics did not emphasize education, and there was the usual contempt expressed for people who had large families they couldn't support and all that, which was more against French-speaking Catholics than the Irish.

My father had a job during the Depression but the situation on the street was terrible. Rents of twelve dollars a month for the flats were paid by the city. The houses weren't heated and kids were always having to run down to the corner store to buy a thirty-cent bag of charcoal. A theme of my mother's was, "If you don't eat your meal, I'll give it to the people next door, the people across the street....."

McGill was anti-French, anti-Catholic and anti-Jewish when I was there as an undergraduate from 1941 to 1945. The first black students came into McGill then, but it wasn't McGill who decided this. The British system was to bring in the bright kids from the colonies in Africa and the West Indies, educate them in England and send them back home to represent British interests. Because of the war, the British universities were occupied with other things. Many of the professors at McGill, including the principal, had all come from British universities. They were called and asked if they would please, because of the war, accept these students at McGill. The first Jewish girl to be allowed into Royal Victoria College, which was the residence, was Victor Goldbloom's sister-in-law from Nova Scotia. When she filled out the form and they saw her religion they said, "We've never had anyone Jewish here." McGill was a very WASP place and they had all kinds of systems to make it difficult for Jews and Catholics to get in. They even set up their own exams to make sure that their kids got in because so many of them were not passing the provincials. This all changed after the war. Veterans came back and had the right to go to university and the universities had no choice but to take in whoever wanted to come. I've always been very interested in other people and other people's lives. At McGill I was very involved with the Cosmopolitan Club and meeting all kinds of people. I thought this was absolutely wonderful and I still think it is. I think Canada is so much improved with all the varied immigrants that come here. My solution to the Irish question is that they should open their doors and take in a couple of thousand immigrants from all the countries of the world so they'd stop hating each other. (laughs) It might be a good solution for some other countries, too.

I don't think of myself as being Irish unless someone talks about it. I'm not a nationalist. I'm not even a Canadian nationalist, although I like Canada better than I used to. I really disliked the old WASP thing. When I was invited to join two women's fraternities at McGill, I refused because I disapproved of them.

I don't know when I started to reject my parents' view of history. I guess it was when I was in high school and started to read a lot. Because I rejected their values, it changed my life. It made me a cynic about everything. If you reject your parents' values you look at everything with a jaundiced eye. Actually, I'm grateful for this. When I travel in Third World countries I observe how important religion is to so many people because it's about the only thing that makes life bearable. But I feel very fortunate that I can live as an atheist. My philosophy of life? I love it. I think I appreciate it much more because I'm an atheist.

I married Phil Cutler, who was Jewish. I had had a Jewish boyfriend earlier and my parents didn't accept him, but later I think they were so happy to get me married, they didn't mind and they quite liked Phil. He was a very exciting, handsome and dramatic sort of person and a brilliant lawyer. He even got a doctorate in law which was very rare. He was a judge when he died. I believe that a lot of intermarriages work better than non-mixed marriages. Certainly, observing my own, things that upset one partner from his own family background and traditions don't upset the other, and vice versa. Two people have to be very much in love when they come from different backgrounds because of the social pressures. The belief that people get along better when they're from their own background is a myth. I have four sons. I had four children in three and a half years. The ones in the middle are twins. My husband wasn't religious either, and so we never had a problem about how to bring up the children.

I visited Ireland only once. My husband was attending a Bar convention in Dublin, I think it was in the eighties. We flew to Shannon, drove to Dublin, then up to Galway and then to Belfast which I thought an ugly city. I'm told that it is typical of nineteenth century British industrial cities like Liverpool and Bristol. It was a depressing place without beauty or any kind of variety that makes life liveable. Anyway, I picked up a newspaper in Belfast and there was a big to-do on the front page. The only Irishman in Northern Ireland to get the Victoria Cross in World War II was a Catholic, and he had just died.* The Protestants in the north are very pro-British and very supportive of the army so the big question was: Was it all right for Orangemen to attend a Mass House (believe it or not, "Mass House") to attend the funeral? The head of the Orange Lodge for Ireland said it was all right to go and attend this funeral. Members of the Lodge were asking for his resignation. I said to Phil, "I don't want to stay here. Let's go back to Dublin."

The Ebbitts were still in Cavan and we visited the house where my father was born. There was even an Ebbitt's Lane. I wasn't too sure about the house where my mother was born because there are no more Protestants left in Leitrim. They had all gone north, presumably to create all the problems in Londonderry that are going on today. We asked an old man walking on the road if he remembered the Farrellys and he said, "They've all gone north." We found the church but we couldn't find my grandparents' graves. The grass was up high over every tomb and the church door was actually ajar and looked like it hadn't been used in years.

I visited one of my father's relatives in Cavan and got such a depressed feeling in their house. The silence, the bitterness and the hardness which is so common in farm life. There's a great deal of nonsensical romanticising of farm life. There were fourteen in my mother's family and the father was so strict the children were not allowed to speak at the table and had to go to bed at nine o'clock at night. My mother told me that when her father caught her brother smoking in the barn he beat him so badly with a hawthorne stick that for several nights afterwards he could be heard moaning from pain. His back was torn to bits from the thorns. Then he left for England and never returned.

I served as mayor of Westmount from 1987 to 1991. I came in as a protest candidate and never expected to win. I was trying to get various people to run for council and they all turned to me and said, "Why don't YOU run for mayor?" Brian Gallery was going in by acclamation as nearly all the mayors had done. There had only been two elections in the whole history of Westmount. Westmount has many traditions and one of them is that four or five months after a new administration takes over, a dinner is held at the University Club where the old and the new can meet each other. They usually have about six wines and everyone makes witty speeches and jokes and so on. At the dinner given for me and the new councillors, one of them said, "When I heard that May Cutler was elected, all I could think of was—another goddamned Irishman." (laughs)

*Leading Seaman James Magennis (Royal Navy) was award the Victoria Cross for attaching limpet mines to a Japanese cruiser under difficult circumstances in Singapore Harbour, July 1945. He moved to England in the 1950s after struggling to earn a living in Belfast.

The Irish Jaunting Car, a fixture in every St. Patrick's Parade
since 1898, carrying O'Neill Splude and Kay Bourbonnais
on March 19, 1944. It was built in 1887 by James Kenehan, Wagon Maker.
Photo by Kay Peachey.

Reverend Thomas D. McEntee, C.M.,C.D.

Father McEntee was born in Griffintown in 1924 and was ordained a diocesan priest in 1954. He is a loved and respected member of the Montreal Irish community and keeps in touch with all the people he knew in Griffintown. The McEntee family lived in what is known as the O'Connell's Block at the corner of Murray and Ottawa. After service in the navy in World War II, he entered the seminary and, upon ordination, served at St. Kevin's, the mission of St. Philip Neri, and then back to St. Kevin's before becoming pastor of St. Edmund of Canterbury in 1974. In 1990, Father McEntee was appointed to the Order of Canada for his involvement in community affairs.

In a lighter vein, in 1991 Father McEntee organized a ghost watch and former Griffintowners and others gathered at the corner of Murray and William Streets to await the appearance of the Headless Woman (Mary Gallagher).

When I was born, my family, my parents, brothers and sisters were living on Ottawa Street at the corner of Murray in O'Connell's block. Thomas O'Connell had lived in the house before us. When he left there and went to live on Mountain Street his house was divided. Mike Noonan and his wife lived below and we had the upstairs. I lived there from 1924 to about 1939. There were about twenty families living in that block. We all knew each other. We knew the people who lived across the road, we knew the people who lived down the street, we knew the people who lived over on Duke Street. We knew all these people relatively intimately, I would say.

Expo year, 1967 was the big change. Goose Village was just simply decimated and a lot of Griffintown was lost to roads and construction. People moved out and that was about the end of it. Where I lived is still there and there are a few houses around but if you ask me what it was like as far as the Irish community was concerned, we just lived in an Irish community. That was it. I can go from street to street and tell you names of people who lived there. You pretty well knew everyone. Our memories are long and we still know each other. There are few, if anyone, who lived in Griffintown that I don't know. I feel quite comfortable going to their wakes and funerals because we were a community. You were very much a part of their lives and they were very much a part of your life. People think I have some kind of fixation on funerals because I'm always at one but I know these people. I was brought up with them.

There was always a little bit of rivalry between Point St. Charles and Griffintown. I guess some people might have thought it was a step up to live in the Point. If anybody moved out of Griffintown, if for instance, they moved to

N.D.G., we used to say that they had moved to Hungry Hill. I suppose the Irish expression would be that they were living beyond their means. They perhaps could pay the rent but couldn't eat. I doubt if it was true but that's what was said. (laughs)

Thomas O'Connell was my uncle. We lived over his plumbing shop where my father was the superintendent. I remember him as being a very distinguished man. I don't think that I had very many words with him. I just knew that he was there and I used to see him in the office. Maybe I was too small and insignificant to be considered but he was always a presence. I remember the time a crucial election speech was given from our balcony which was very small and looked out over the intersection of Ottawa and Murray Streets. Doctor Conroy made the statement that if Thomas O'Connell weren't elected that everyone would eat snowballs that winter. He was, of course, elected. He served for thirty-two consecutive years and was known as the Dean of City Council. I know that they were very charitable people. His wife, Mary Jane, was my father's sister and I was told that it wasn't uncommon for Mrs. O'Connell to bring grocery orders to the poor during the Depression.

We used to walk in the St. Patrick's Parade and I can remember being lined up. Mind you, we didn't have the sophistication that we have today in removing the snow so, for little tykes like myself the snow could be up to your knees. One time I remember being lined up on Windsor Street right opposite the New Carlton Hotel, which was located near the old Mother Martin's Restaurant, when some insult about the Pope was yelled down at us from the top window. The parade just emptied itself as everyone ran into the hotel. I don't think they got very far inside but they were ready to avenge the slurs that had been made. There were also smart alecks who would throw money at you in the parade and, as a little child, you would stoop down and pick up the money and then, of course, cause a tumble. They'd try these sorts of things, you know. I can't even rationalize these actions today. I just know that it was done and it was mean.

Every spring, the St. Ann's Young Men's Society would organize a street race. The streets would be blocked off and the fellows would line up, just like you see in the Olympics today. They would have races according to different ages and would grant trophies to the winners. I'm not a sports person but I remember my older brother Frank winning a trophy.

In the summer we'd play ball on the street and if a ball (we mostly played with tennis balls) went down a sewer, you'd take the sewer cover off and there were always a couple of brave guys who would go down the sewer and rescue the

Tom McEntee during World War II.
"I was in the navy and so was my brother Frank.
I have great, fond memories of the war year."
Courtesy of Reverend Thomas McEntee.

ball. That was nothing that I would want to do. We also played hopscotch and chestnuts. We'd go to Mount Royal and get chestnuts. We'd harden them and put a cord through them and then try to break the other person's chestnut. And alleys, marbles. There were always prize marbles, ones that would knock out the others. We would start in the spring and, of course, you could even play in the winter by making holes in the snow. We also played in the back yards or would go to the park on Basin Street which was quite popular for sports. Some of the teenagers would play handball against the bricks of the fire station on the corner of Eleanor and Ottawa Streets. Captain Mullins was there for years and he ran a very tight ship. The men used to line up for inspection and the engines and everything were spotless. There was a lane behind the plumbing shop and my dad put a shower there. We would all get our bathing suits on and jump around under the shower because there were no pools except for O'Connell's Bath on Haymarket Square which was a popular place. There had also been a Gallery's Bath but it had disappeared by my time.

In the winter, the snow was ploughed away from the buildings and from the center of the street forming snowbanks along the curbs. We all cleared a path from our homes to the street and it was a great thing for kids. We could play cowboys and Indians along the snowbanks. You could jump across every opening as if you were jumping over a ravine just as you would see it in the movies.

Another part of our life was Borden's Milk. It was a milk company and it was right on Murray Street so very early in the morning the milkman would be up and you could hear the clanking of the glass bottles. We also had blacksmiths. I remember at least two blacksmith shops on William Street. You could pass by there and see the blacksmith shoeing a horse. There was a fish and chips store and, of course, traditionally, the fish was wrapped in newspaper. There was also a Chinese laundry on Murray Street and the kids used to tease the Chinese laundry man and he would come out of his shop and run up Murray Street after them with his iron in his hand.

The St. Ann's Young Men's Society building was on the corner of Young and Ottawa and right beside that building, as you walked up Young, was the Christian Brothers' Residence and St. Ann's Boys' School. The school yard behind the school opened on to Colborne Street and when we were in the school yard we could run out on to Colborne Street and grab the yeast that was coming out of the flue of the brewery in blobs. The brave ones would eat it.

Of course, you didn't get into the movies then. Children weren't allowed in on account of the Laurier Theatre fire but if you knew Dinny Mahoney who was Captain Mahoney's son, then you might get in. Dinny and I were great friends. Captain Mahoney was the captain of the fire station on Chaboillez Square. Dinny and I used to be able to get into Fairyland Theatre because we had passes. I'd give anything to know where Dinny Mahoney is today. I'm still searching for him. I lost track of him during the war years so I don't know if he's alive or dead today.

The Griffintown Boys' Club was rather controversial. It was a product of Red Feather and, of course, was Protestant. Everyone belonged to it. I joined the Wolf Cubs there and eventually Boy Scouts. When Father O'Hara came to the parish (I'm repeating what I was told) he said that we couldn't go there because it was a Protestant Club. At Christmas, for example, (remember, we are talking about an area where many people were on welfare) you'd go to the club, they'd have a Christmas party and you'd come home with gifts. My sister, Dorothy, who was teaching at St. Ann's Kindergarten at the time, just ignored the ruling and let her children go. Dorothy was strong-willed as well so she wasn't to be told because she thought there was nothing wrong with the club. It had a library and was a fantastic place, really. Finally, Father O'Hara went to the club and went through the library and after that the whole thing died out. No one ever stopped going to the club because of him but, unfortunately, he came in like a new broom in the parish. Everyone loved him but he arrived, I suppose, with his own prejudices. I would say that the club has had more of an influence on my life than anything else because of the executive director, Cyril Dendy, who was an Anglican. And you may know Cliff Sowery. Cliff succeeded Cyril Dendy and was a boxer. Boxing was the big forte of the Griffintown Boys' Club and they produced many notable fighters. We had a gymnasium there and all sorts of crafts. And dentistry—I used to go and have my teeth attended to for nothing. The only thing that cost you five cents was an extraction.

My father always worked during the Depression so we were fortunate, I guess. Besides his work with the Thomas O'Connell company, he owned horses and had men working for him in the Corporation. The horses would be brought into the back yard, be unharnessed and put into the stable. The next morning the men would be up and out again to clean and sand the streets or whatever they had to do at that time. I can remember talk of people surviving on molasses and bread, that sort of thing. At school, you knew by the appearance of some children that they were poor. There was this boy from the Village who was always getting in trouble in school because he never had a haircut. I can remember one time (I was only in first or second grade) asking my parents if I couldn't get him a haircut. My parents sprung the money which let me get him a haircut from the barber on Murray Street. There were people who were very, very poor. My mother used to speak of people as being "on relief." She was a person who helped a lot and when Father Gordon McGuinness, who was frequently in our home, came she would give him clothes to give to poor families. The problem was that the clothes belonged to my sisters and when they would come home to look for them they would be gone. It was a sore point but was a standing joke in our house.

The Redemptorist Fathers were very visible. You saw them in the schools and in the street. The church was the center of your life at the time and the priests would visit your home. My first recollection of them was in connection with my First Communion. I had pursued the possibility of becoming a Redemptorist and might very well have if somebody had taken a little interest in me at the time. They seemed to live a semi-monastic life. For instance, you'd go to the rectory or the office and there would be a sign, Cloister, so you never went beyond that sign. There were a lot of priests because they were there for their novitiate (a probationary period in a religious order.) I can recall that there were six confessionals and you could go in, let's say, on a Saturday and you would find six priests hearing confessions but there were no lineups so that there was a lot of service given to you. It seems to me that everyone who was a Catholic went to church although in school on Monday mornings you'd be questioned as to whether you went to Mass and there were always some that never went. Many of those were from the Village which meant coming across the canal which was difficult in the winter although the authorities would put up barges with railings so that the people living in the Village could take a shortcut across the canal rather than come via the bridge or through the tunnel which would have been very long in the cold.

The big thing with St. Ann's was the devotions to Our Mother of Perpetual Help. They were so popular that they began to run a bus line from Ogilvy's on St. Catherine Street right down Mountain which ran into McCord below St. James Street. They started early in the morning with devotions throughout the day until 9:15 at night. Protestants and Catholics came from all over, especially after work, to the very popular devotions. We're talking thousands of people "making the Tuesdays." There was a beautiful shrine with crutches and other signs of cures and things like that around it. There were some very able preachers there. Some of those Redemptorists just captivated you.

My family were Conservatives until Frank Connors, my cousin, ran for office and then the family switched and became Liberal. Frank Connors married my cousin, Irene O'Connell. He was a chemist and never lived in Griffintown. He had a drugstore on Notre Dame Street at the top of Murray called McGale's. He was a member of the Legislative Assembly and after his death he was succeeded by Frank Hanley. Frank was a popular politician because he was a man of the people. He used to sing and dance and I can remember him tap dancing once on the top of a piano. When there weren't too many automobiles he used to drive a yellow roadster which was either a Chev or a Ford, I forget which.

The first death that I remember from the war was a fellow named Robert Pitts who was from the Village and had joined the air force. He had been a scout with me and his death affected me greatly. I was in the navy and so was my brother Frank. After ordination, I rejoined the RCN as a reserve chaplain and served long enough to receive the long service medal, the Canada Decoration. I have great, fond memories of the war years. There's a great camaraderie in the forces.

Before the war, Cyril Dendy (who had left the Griffintown Boys' Club and was now executive director of the Boy Scouts) asked me if I would like to go to work for the Boy Scouts. I worked for them for a couple of years as quartermaster on Bishop Street. After the war I worked in industry for a while and then I pursued the possibility of the seminary. The Department of Veterans' Affairs gave us the opportunity of studying so I went down to Boston to a school for delayed vocations and studied there for one year to bring my high school credits up to scratch (I was a high school dropout) so that I could enter a regular academic system.

I entered the Seminary of Philosophy and, after two years I went to the Grand Seminary. I spent a quarter of a year there but, unfortunately, I'm not bilingual and I felt swamped there so I petitioned to be allowed to go to an English Seminary but I wasn't successful. I was sent to St. Paul's in Ottawa which taught in Latin, strangely enough, and was run by the Oblates. It was bilingual in the sense that you would ask your question in the vernacular and the answer came back in Latin so, French or English, you asked your question but you got your answer in Latin so that everybody got the benefit of the answer. All announcements were in French and English so it was my salvation.

I was only the second man to study outside the diocese and it wasn't easy. Originally, I had wanted to be a Redemptorist but, at that time, they were being sent to the missions for a period of time. That wasn't my forte so I told Cardinal

Léger, the archbishop of Montreal, that I wasn't surviving in French and that I might just as well say goodbye to Montreal. I wanted to go to London, Ontario or St. Augustine's in Scarborough to study and, with a heave and a sigh, Cardinal Léger agreed and St. Paul's in Ottawa was the compromise.

Archbishop Charbonneau was very well-liked. He was the one who gave the English clergy permission to wear suits on the street. Before that we wore cassocks. Archbishop Charbonneau was from Ontario and he came to Quebec as archbishop of one of the most prestigious, if not the largest diocese in Canada. Obviously where he came from he wore a suit on the street and I think he could understand the thinking of the English priests. Times were changing and there was also the American influence. I remember very well when he left Quebec. I was in the seminary at the time and I went to see Father Clement Locas, who was my spiritual director. He was a Sulpician who used to come down to St. Gabriel's on Sundays to say Mass and who had interviewed me before I went to the seminary. He was a nice man who had helped me a lot and I respected him. When I went in the radio was on in his room which was very unusual because Sulpicians, at that time, lived very strictly and a radio on in his room was really a surprise. His word to me was, "I'm waiting to hear the announcement of our new bishop." That stunned me and I said, "What happened to the old one?" He said, "He's resigned and he's in British Columbia." It came as a shock to everyone that Archbishop Charbonneau was gone. *

*In 1949 the Quebec government of Maurice Duplessis, legislated a comprehensive labour code which was intended to suppress growing labour union activity, including the illegal strike of the CTCC (Conféderation des Travailleurs Catholiques du Canada) against the Johns-Manville Company in Asbestos, Quebec. Duplessis denounced the union leadership and sent in his Provincial Police. Archbishop Roy of Quebec City, Bishop Desranleau of Sherbrooke and Bishop Douville of Saint-Hyacinthe supported the strikers and sent aid to the asbestos workers and their families. Their support was rather cautious when compared with Archbishop Joseph Charbonneau of Montreal. In a sermon in Notre Dame Basilica he declared:

> The working class is the victim of a conspiracy which wishes to crush it, and when there is a conspiracy to crush the working class, it is the duty of the Church to intervene.

Duplessis, with the aid of conservative Jesuits led by Bishop Courchèsne of Rimouski, was successful in having Archbishop Charbonneau exiled to Victoria, British Columbia. (Source: *The Confederation of National Trade Unions Yesterday and Today*, Black Rose Books, Montreal, 1972).

Leo Leonard

Leo Leonard, aka Claw-Hammer Jack, operates a stable in Griffintown. What was once a common way of life has now become folklore and a visit to his Griffintown Horse Palace is a fascinating trip back in time. Leo graciously shows his stable and horses to anyone who is interested. There is no denying his great love of horses. This interview took place on a grey November afternoon in 1991 in the tack room behind his house on Ottawa Street. The skyscrapers of downtown Montreal were visible but seemed very remote from this gentle, slow-paced life. As we spoke, some of the drivers returned with their calèches and as they drove by the window it was easy to imagine oneself back fifty years ago. His completely renovated house retains its original look from the outside. To reach the stable one walks by the side of the house, which in summer is a flower-lined path, right through to the stable on the left. Immediately behind his house is a separate building which contains the tack room with a stove to provide warmth on a chilly day.

I was born on Forfar Street in Goose Village on May 5, 1926. It was a good neighbourhood, all Irish and Italian. My mother was half-Irish and half-French and my father was Irish. I went to the St. Ann's Kindergarten for one year and one of the teachers was Sister Louise. She was a wonderful woman. She died recently at 103 years of age. She was very, very nice. She had an awful gang to deal with. We did all crazy things, teasing girls and everything else but she looked after us very well. When I went to St. Ann's Boys' School I had Brother Arthur, a hell of a hockey player and ball player. Brother Patrick taught everybody. He was there for about sixty years. The brothers made us learn. Very tough. If you didn't listen to them and you wanted to fight, they could fight with you. All the brothers played hockey, handball and baseball with the boys and they could teach you a lot about sports. My father went to St. Ann's too. I was married in St. Ann's Church by Father Baldwin.

I got interested in horses because of the Furlong family which kept horses in Goose Village. I've known the Furlongs for fifty years and I was always there when I was a kid. William Furlong Senior taught me a lot about horses and then when I was old enough I drove a wagon delivering ice for them. I got my nickname Claw-Hammer from one of the Furlong brothers when I was a young guy and it stuck all these years. Most of my friends use it. I also drove a carriage for Leo Feron. I worked for the City cleaning snow and then I went into the shipyard business for about twenty years and then back into the horse business. I was always a good horseman. They're wonderful animals. They listen to you and they're good to work with. They're very smart and can even untie knots. A lot of horses don't get along with one another. You have to separate them so they can't kick each other. They fight with their feet. I've been kicked lots of times. It feels like you've been punched. I've been kicked in the stomach and the legs by mistake, you know. They don't do it intentionally.

During World War II I quit the horses to work in the Montreal Dry Dock, Vickers. I was a rivet heater, the guy who heats the rivets for the riveter. I worked there all during the war and later, until 1950 or 1951. Then I worked as a waiter in the Belmont Tavern on the corner of Bridge and Wellington. Five years in there and from there to the wharf for twenty years. I'm retired now. I've had the horses since I started working on the wharf. I liked that work and I wish I were still there. I was a cooper. That's the guy who repairs broken boxes. Seventy or eighty percent of the guys were French. We got along very well. I was a very good friend of Gus Mell, the boxer. We worked together on the wharf for about twelve years. He was fifty-eight when he died.

I don't have a favourite horse. I like them all and we don't kill them or shoot them or anything. We retire them here or we find a farm to take them for not too much money. Sandy's retired and the pony's retired. Sandy is twenty-seven years old and the pony is twenty-eight. The pony went in the St. Patrick's Parade for twenty-one years—drove all my nieces and nephews and the Clahane kids. Most of the people who rode the pony are married today. Some of them have children of their own.

I moved from Goose Village to Westmount and then when I renovated this house I moved down beside the stable so I could look after the horses. That was in 1984. My house was originally bought by the Martin Kiely family in 1862. That's as far back as we can read the papers, the others are faded too much. Just some of the wood remains from the old structure which had to be left there. When they took the old bricks off there was wood underneath so they put bricks over the wooden house. This place at one time was a livery stable. People would come from out of town and they could leave their horses and sleep in this house. This tack room used to be the bunk house. This building too comes from Martin Kiely. Nobody lives in this house but it came with the property. I started renting this place from him twenty-five years ago and then I bought it ten years ago and rebuilt the house in front.

We have a few horses that board here. We do a lot of the horse care ourselves. We've been in the business a long time so we know when a horse is sick and we fix him up. If we need a veterinarian, he comes here. The horse-shoers come by truck from St. Hyacinthe or St. Jean to shoe them. There are also a lot of them between here and Ottawa. I have a man who comes in the morning and straightens everything. He feeds the horses and cleans the stable. He comes back at five o'clock at night. He lives uptown on Drummond Street. He used to be around Dominion Square all the time minding the horses when the drivers had to go to the bathroom or eat. I asked him if he wanted a job and he said yes. The drivers brush their horses but I clean my own. This is the last stable in Montreal. The closest one is across the bridge. And we have all the gardeners who take our manure away for their gardens, Italian, French, Irish, German. They take it in the spring. We have enough space to hold it until then. If we're overloaded we get a truck to take it away. The neighbours don't say anything. They are mostly people from all over the city, people who work in night clubs and want to be close to their work. Some of them work at McGill and others work with the carriages.

We have all kinds of horses: trotters, pacers, Percherons, carriage horses, what they call road horses and that's it. If anything is wrong with a horse from Blue Bonnets and he can't make the speed any more after ten or twelve years, you can buy them for the carriage business. We never lost a horse in this stable. We've had a few small accidents, a broken wheel or something like that. I never had a horse killed or had a carriage demolished. There was a lot of ice in the streets in the old days but today we have shoes on them that are good all year round just like tires on a car. The horses never slip with these shoes. The blacksmith comes every six weeks and renews them or fixes them. The horses work every day of the week in the summer when it's nice. On rainy days they don't work. I don't feel they work too hard. Sixty years ago the horses never went home because it was too hot. They went out and worked. Human beings work. At eighty degrees a horse can still work but don't keep him out too long. A horse should only work eight or nine hours.

As long as the tourists keep coming to the city there will be work for carriage drivers but with all the laws we have now tourism isn't doing so well. We never had to fire anybody or tell them to get out because of mistreating a horse. If they want to mistreat a horse we don't hire them. If they drink or take dope we get rid of them. I'm getting ready to retire. I feel old. I haven't got any kids and some of the drivers that I have would buy the place tomorrow if I wanted to sell it. Most of these young guys had fathers who were in the business. They grew up in the business. They had to pass their test from the City and they make their living driving carriages. It's an English and French test and you've got to know the city like a taxi driver. They've got to have a pocket number to drive. The owners of the horses have to make sure they can handle them. You can drive with me to learn but you go to pass your test with the City. It costs eighty dollars a year to keep your number.

I'd like to see more people move to Griffintown but there aren't many houses here. At night there aren't too many people. A lot of bicycle riders pass through from the bicycle path on the Lachine Canal. That's all we see. Only Joe Neeson lives here. The O'Donnells and the O'Connells have their businesses here. They're all friends of mine. There aren't many stores here so people need a car or they walk to the corner of Peel and Ottawa and get on the bus and go uptown. It takes two minutes. Everyone knows one another. Everyone likes one another. Nobody has any trouble. I can also go to Point St. Charles to see my friends. Everyone in Point St. Charles knows me. I see my friends at Mama's Tavern on Centre Street and at the Capri on St. Patrick Street. That belongs to a Frenchman but a lot of the boys go there.

The services we provide today are the carriages for driving tourists on Dominion Square and in Old Montreal. We also do weddings and retirements. We do them all. The only place to have a sleigh ride now is on Mount Royal. You have to make a reservation and fix it up with the driver. I'm too old to ride now. I have to settle with driving once in a while. When I haven't got a driver I'll go out and drive myself. I have three of my own horses, the rest are boarders. Like I said; I don't have a favourite. I like them all.

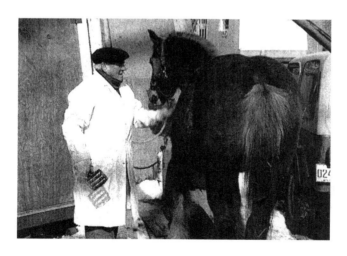

Leo Leonard at his Griffintown House Palace.
Courtesy of Richard Burman.

Patricia McDonnell McLeod

Patricia McLeod was born in Griffintown in 1927. She was married in St. Ann's Church to Jimmy McLeod whom she met when he came into her father's store to buy Chiclets. Her parents were born in Montreal but her grandparents were born in Ireland. She is the granddaughter of John Taugher, the lacrosse player. Her sister Margaret joined the Sisters of Charity.

My mother and father had a store for twenty-three years on the corner of Wellington and McCord. It was called McDonnell's. My father enlarged the store when they started to build the Wellington Tunnel. That was in the early thirties, I think. It was a very small store when my father took it over, just a corner store. It was a two-storey building and the store was downstairs. We used to live at the back of the store. John Killoran and his wife lived upstairs. He was an enormous man, a blacksmith and he was very, very strong. He had the strength of maybe three men.

My father expanded the store because of the demand from the men who were building the tunnel—they used to work three shifts around the clock. They would come over and ask if they could have sandwiches and coffee so my father got the idea to make a restaurant. That's when we moved upstairs. Before that it was a general store that sold cigarettes, cigars, milk, bread, and biscuits and candy in those big jars.

My sister and I used to serve and help out which we hated doing when we were young. Later, when I worked for Bell Telephone, I'd have to serve when I came home because the store was open from six in the morning till midnight. It was a long day, seven days a week, and we were expected to help out, which we did—not always willingly but we did. My parents really loved having the store. They would complain about being tired but at night the restaurant became a gathering place for all the older men in the neighbourhood. My grandmother lived up the street and sometimes at night my mother and my aunt used to go there and knit. Tuesday was always a busy day in the restaurant because of the Tuesday devotions at St. Ann's across the street. People would drop in after the services to have toast and coffee or a sandwich.

It was on a Tuesday morning on April 25th, 1944 when the plane crashed in Griffintown. People had just come out of the 9:30 service in the morning and the store was packed. I was home at the time because I had a leave of absence from work because my mother was in the hospital and I was helping out. This plane came flying overhead and it was flying so low it was below the steeple of

St. Ann's Church. When it flew over it was making such a racket that all the windows were rattling and everybody got so scared. We knew there was something wrong and we all ran out to see. The plane flew past and went up toward the Lachine Canal and for some unknown reason, it turned back. It flew back over our place and when it got to Colborne Street, which was only a couple of streets away, one of the wings fell off and the plane crashed into a whole block of houses. Miss Keegan, a nurse with the Victorian Order of Nurses, happened to be in the store having coffee. She said, "Come with me, quickly." We ran and got there before the police or anybody. You could see inside the plane. They were all burned; there wasn't anything left. It was all smoke and fire; it was a terrible mess, I can tell you that. Pretty near a whole block of houses was demolished and ten or twelve people were killed. Everybody was pretty sad about the people dying. It all happened so fast.

Sometimes there would be as many as thirty priests at St. Ann's because the Redemptorists were a missionary order and when they would finish preaching, they would come and stay at their residence on Basin Street. They all used to come over to the store for a cup of coffee. When my sister and I were quite young, Father Fee, who was a huge man, would come in. He always had indigestion and he'd say to my mother, "Please fix me a Bromo Seltzer." Mother would fix it up and we'd sit and watch him. He'd take one mouthful and he'd sing, "I'm Forever Blowing Bubbles."We used to pray that he'd have indigestion because we loved to hear him sing.

We lived on the corner, right across from the church so, in the summertime, we were allowed to stay out maybe till 9:30 at night as long as we stayed right outside the door. They were very strict in those days. We'd be out playing with some of our friends who lived close by. Father Baines and this other priest used to walk around Griffintown every night and make the rounds. Father Baines had a cane and he'd come along and say, "Pat McDonnell, you get in the house. It's after nine o'clock," and he'd whack you on your ankles with his cane. Father Kearney was so popular and so loved by everyone that we used to call him Father Honey. I remember going to Confession one time when I was around twelve. I went to Father Kearney—"Father, I accuse myself of...." and he said, "Is that you Patsy?" I never went to him after that.

My mother drove a car, a Plymouth. There would be so many wakes up at Feron's on St. Antoine Street in those days—1937-38, that the priest would ask my mother to drive him. My mother would respond, "Yes Father, as long as you

Bill McDonnell standing behind the counter of McDonnell's store
on the corner of McCord (Mountain) and Wellington in the 1930s.
The store was later renamed the Coffee Pot and was a popular
place to meet your friends after Mass or a Tuesday devotion
service at St. Ann's Church across the street.
Courtesy of Patricia McLeod.

promise when you're at the wake you only say one decade of the beads, not the whole rosary, because I've got rheumatism in my knees." He'd promise faithfully and when they'd get there he'd say the whole rosary and then my mother would say to the priest, "After this, don't come and ask me any more."

A lot of people who lived in Goose Village had their funerals at St. Ann's. Many of them were Italians. They would march through the Wellington Tunnel with their own bands and after the funeral, they would march with the band behind the hearse as far as Notre Dame Street. From the store we would see that some of the women became so hysterical that they had to be carried out of the church. They would be brought over to the store for some refreshment.

About 230 meals a day were served in our restaurant. My father would work at the cash and my mother would help around with the waitresses. It was hard to keep cooks—we had eight in four years. We had a lot of funny cooks, I can tell you that. One of the drawbacks of a restaurant is that when the men came to deliver the soft drinks, they would come in the back entrance and leave the door open. There were a lot of rats around because the restaurant was near the canal with all the grain sheds. I mean, they were really big, healthy rats so it was not unusual for a rat to get into the kitchen and my father and Howard Quesnel, who worked for Zenith Tire, would each get a broom and they'd go into the kitchen and close off the two doors and they would get the rat. One particular time the rat got into a cupboard near a pipe. my father went to give it a whack and we always heard never to corner a rat. The rat came out and my father said that he stood on his hind legs and jumped for his throat but landed on his shoulder. From that day on, my father would never go near a rat. That really finished him. Some time after that another rat got into the kitchen. Now what were we going to do? My father didn't want to have anything to do with it. There was a woman called Mrs. Doody who lived on Basin Street. She told my father that she would get her dog Lilly to kill the rat. My father said, "Mrs. Doody, do you have any idea how big this rat is? It's a big sewer rat." Anyway, she landed over with Lilly, a tiny little white dog. "This is Lilly. She'll kill the rat." My father said, "The rat's going to kill the dog. There's no way." She said, "You don't know my Lilly." So he took her word for it, put the dog in the kitchen and closed the door. About five minutes later, we heard scratching on the door. My father opened the door and the dog came out proud as anything. The rat was dead just like a surgeon had done it, as neat as anything. She was a real little rat killer. Every time there was a rat in the store, my father would say, "Go and ask Mrs. Doody." She would get a couple of dollars for every rat.

Griffintown was a grand neighbourhood. The houses didn't have galleries so everybody would sit outside on their doorstep in the summer. The people upstairs would lean on the windowsill looking out and as you walked up the street, you knew everybody and they knew you. It was a wonderful place to be because you just felt at home no matter where you were in Griffintown. If any woman got sick all the other ladies would go and cook her meals for her or bring meals to her. Everybody helped everybody. It was really wonderful. You never locked your door down there. No way. You just didn't.

One Sunday morning after Mass, I came up McCord Street and along Ottawa Street to go and call on a friend of mine. Borden's had their place on Murray Street and all their horses and wagons were there. They used to deliver milk on Sundays too, of course. I was walking along and I heard this very unusual noise behind me. I didn't know what it was. Luckily, I jumped into a doorway. It was a runaway horse that had escaped from the stables and he ran clear along Ottawa Street and ran right into the Lachine Canal. That was the end of the horse. (laughs)

The priests at St. Ann's were so good to the poor. They were just fantastic. There was a family with about seven or eight children who lived on Murray Street and they weren't Catholic but they were very poor. They never seemed to have enough food and the priests used to bring food over to them. They never forgot the poor. They kept in such close contact with the families that they knew when there was a problem so they would be there to help. It's not like that anymore.

I know of some cases where the husband would get paid on Friday and not come home with his pay. He'd go to some tavern and then the wife would just get in touch with the priest, Father Maguire especially. He was a huge man, a big, strong Irishman and he would go to the tavern, grab hold of him and he'd drag him home to the wife.

St. Patrick's Day was always a big day in the store and every year we used to sell shamrocks, maybe 500 pots, and we had to water them every day. Then the men would all come into the store the day of the parade to get their beaver hats trimmed with shamrocks. We were very busy trimming them and then we'd rush out to see the parade. The St. Ann's men always looked so grand in the parade.

We lived near the Redpath Sugar Company on Bridge Street. Most people that we knew would get a big bag of sugar from Redpath and then use the bags to make dishtowels. The women would bleach them and get all the print out of them. There was a Mrs. Hardy who lived on McCord who used to make her bloomers out of the sugar bags. All the women stayed home in those days and Monday was washday, Tuesday was ironing day. So, on washday—all the women would be hanging their clothes on the line—there would be ten lines in one place. Mrs. Hardy would put her washing out with all her bloomers and right on the seat of the pants it said: LET REDPATH SWEETEN IT.

Down in Griffintown if somebody died, some of the women would go to the widow's house and sit up all night with the body. People didn't go to the funeral parlour at all. It was all done in the home. When Mrs. Hardy's husband died, Mrs. Brennan, my mother and another woman went to Mrs. Hardy's house that night. "Now, don't worry. We're going to sit up with you all through the night. You won't be alone here." "Oh," says Mrs. Hardy, "I'm not sitting up. When ten o'clock comes you're all getting out of here. Didn't you notice I haven't been crying at all?" They *had* noticed it but they didn't say anything. They thought she must be in a state of shock. "I never cry," she says, "because I break out in blotches and tomorrow is the funeral and I want my complexion to be beautiful." (laughs)

One time there was a funeral at St. Ann's. I can't remember who it was but Rocket (Maurice) Richard came to it and this was when he was a really big star. In those days, the men would come into the store and listen to the hockey games. They'd all sit around on these stools just listening and, boy, they were great fans. My father was crazy about the Rocket and so was everybody else. After the funeral, the Rocket came into the restaurant. Well! He went to get served at the counter and the waitresses were all excited. You know, the Rocket! The waitress asked him for his autograph and he said, "Yes, certainly." At that time, my sister was working over at the cash and when he finished whatever he had he came over to pay his bill. He took a picture of himself out of his pocket which he had signed for this waitress. He gave it to my sister and she said, "I don't want that," and she gave it back to him. (laughs) My father nearly killed her. He said, "You insulted the Rocket. He'll never come back in this place." She said, "I'm not a hockey fan, what do I want his picture for?"

One man who used to come to the restaurant to listen to the hockey games was sitting there one night. The game was being broadcast in French and, when it was over, this man said to my father, "Boy, that guy Larondelle, he was all over the ice tonight. He must be a terrific player. He's a new guy, I guess." (Note: *la rondelle* is French for puck)

I'll always be happy that I had the experience of growing up in Griffintown.

The people were so warm and friendly and you were never lonesome. You could go to anybody's place and you knew that you were always welcome. They were mostly big families and there was lots of fun. The families didn't need anybody else because they could have so much fun by themselves. The Church played a big part. They gave you such a good foundation for your faith and I can still remember some of those sermons today. When you listened to a sermon at St. Ann's, you remembered it for the rest of the week.

Jim McLeod standing outside McDonnell's store in 1946.
Jim went to the store every morning to buy Chiclets and ended
up marrying Patricia, the owner's daughter.
Courtesy of Patricia McLeod.

Cyril Fisher

Cy Fisher retired from the MUC Police Department in March of 1993 after forty-one years of service. He began his career as a traffic officer in the Town of Mount Royal in 1952. Mayor Vera Danyluk said of him, "He's not a policeman, he's a friend and one of T.M.R.'s finest." Born in Point St. Charles in 1930, he is the prototype of the kind, understanding Irish cop.

My grandmother always wore black because her husband was electrocuted at the age of forty. He was coming home from work for lunch one day and he tried to save two men who had fallen under a crane. Whenever she went shopping she wore black clothes and she'd say to the person, "I'm a widow, you know." Her son James would say, "Ma, they can tell." She'd say, "I want so many carrots and this and that." The man would say, "That will be $1.25, Mrs. Curtis." "Oh, no, you're a thief. I'm a widow, you know." And he ended up giving it to her for fifty cents. When my grandmother was up in years, she'd give me two dollars and say, "Get me six nice pork chops, ten pounds of potatoes, one pound of pork sausages. I also want a pound of butter and a package of tea. Get me a dozen apples and a nice cake." I'd say, "Grandma, I have two dollars." She'd say, "That's enough." (laughs)

I was born on Grand Trunk, right across from the old No. 15 Fire Station on Hibernia Road. I went to Canon O'Meara Elementary School and then I went to Sarsfield School at the corner of Centre and Richmond. It doesn't exist any more. It's a senior citizens' home and a post office now.

I'm Irish through and through. My dad played professional lacrosse for the Shamrocks. He was born in St. Mary's Parish and there was a strong element of Irish there in those days. He worked for the Black Horse Brewery down on Colborne Street which became Dow Brewery which became O'Keefe. There were a lot of Irish people working there. In those days the brewery had beautiful, big Belgian stallions that they used to haul the barrels and the cases of beer. My dad worked six days a week for seventeen dollars. With this he had to feed a family of two girls and two boys. There was always a cousin around who wasn't able to find work and if there weren't enough beds, he'd lie down on the floor.

The company would give picnics and we would look forward to going. We'd ask, "Ma, is it going to rain tomorrow?" The train would bring us from Point St. Charles over to Otterburn Park so it was a thrill just getting on the train. We'd have box lunches with all kinds of sandwiches, ice cream and soft drinks. The prizes were bicycles and money. In those days these were good prizes. They had races and games and they used to have tents with nurses in case somebody got sunstroke. We used to love that picnic. It was always in July and there was no cost to go. Unfortunately there was lots for the adults to drink too. There was a group that got into a boat and they crossed the river. The boat tipped coming back and a girl was drowned so the company stopped the picnics.

My dad was at the brewery right up to the day he retired. There was no Medicare in those days and the company had its own doctor. If there was anyone sick at home, they'd visit the home. They paid for my mother's surgery at the Montreal General Hospital. They looked after you if you had to have teeth extracted or needed glasses. They paid the bill if you had to go to the hospital so it was a good company to work for. Don't forget, we're talking about the Depression years. Everyone was proud to work there because jobs were hard to find in those days.

My dad was a good athlete. If you played lacrosse, you got five dollars a game and they gave you a job for life with the city or, in his case, at Black Horse Brewery. I used to watch him run at the picnics. He was a big man. He didn't smoke cigarettes but once in a while he'd light up a cigar. He'd have a few beers a day but, to be able to run like that, he had to be very good. In those days, lacrosse was our national sport. Field lacrosse was really rough and that's why they stopped playing it. Box lacrosse was similar to hockey but it faded away when hockey became more popular.

My mother told me that when I was only a little pup they used to bring me over to Kahnawake and put me in bed. The Indian women used to take care of me and feed me. They'd set a lovely table and serve a hot meal for everyone after the lacrosse game. The Mohawks were rough during the game but after the game they shook hands and whatever you wanted to eat you got. They were very nice. I've got nothing against the Indians. I think they're great people. I think they've been ripped off.

I entered the Police Force because we were told, "Get a job with security," In those days education was limited because of the cost behind it. Dad would say, "It's fine to work at Northern Electric or Sherwin-Williams but they work on contract." You'd get a contract for three or four years and then there would be a layoff.

We used to have French names like Lamarche and Lefevebre walking in the St. Patrick's Parade with us. They went to Canon O'Meara School so we grew up with French and English. The people who lived next door, the Lacroixs, she could hardly talk any English and my mother couldn't talk any French. Mr.

Lacroix and my dad used to take a beer at night but women weren't allowed into the taverns. There were nineteen taverns and three clubs in the Point. They'd go to a tavern after a hard day's work and they'd talk about politics and sports, have a few beers and come home. Sometimes they'd come home tired and a little bit cross and they'd get a little rowdy raising their voices. It was all tubs, no electric washers, in those days. My mother'd be hanging out clothes and Mrs. Lacroix'd be hanging them out too and she'd say in French, "Madame Fisher, (she'd raise her hands) the big one, your husband, did he come home?" My mother would go, "And your...(with her hands gesturing a short man) ...?" "*Même chose.* I'm getting fed up."(she would make a gesture). People got along very well. If there was a sickness, Madame Lacroix would bring in soup or cookies. It was wonderful how people cared for each other in those days. If you had a telephone everybody would be lined up to use it.

We had to go to church whether you liked it or not. If you weren't there at nine o'clock Mass your name was marked down and Brother Irenaeus would say on Monday morning, "Were you at Mass?" I'd say yes because a lot of times we didn't get up because there was no fire in the stove. The coal would run out and we had to wait until my dad got his pay. This is true. My mother'd say, "Stay in bed. You'll get pneumonia." I'd ask my friend Kenny, "Who served Mass on Sunday?" Kenny would go because he had lots of coal. (laughs) He'd tell me that it was Father Sutton. Brother would ask me who served mass and I would say, "Father Sutton." Brother would say, "Come up here and hold out your hand. It was Father Bracken." Kenny would be there with a big grin on his face.

Brother Irenaeus wore a wig and he had two of them, a red one and a black one. He'd wear the red one on the weekend and the black one during school hours. One windy day, it blew off. We were walking down from church and it was rolling down the street and everybody was laughing and laughing. He was saying, "You saucy pups. Don't laugh. Retrieve me wig. Don't laugh. It could happen to anybody. Wait till you get older." So somebody grabbed the wig and brought it to him. He was a very proud man and that hurt him deeply. He thought we didn't know he had a wig. After that he held his hand on his head when he walked down the street on a windy day.

Sometimes an aunt would say, "We're going to have a little party. We want you to come. You don't have to bring anything." But somebody would always bring something. The women would drink ginger ale and have tea and they'd make cheese and ham sandwiches and cakes and for a dollar you'd get six quarts of beer. There was nearly always a piano in every home in those days and people would get around the piano and sing, tell jokes and laugh. And, you know, they'd go home around maybe twelve or one o'clock in the morning but nobody missed work the next day.

People got along wonderfully but there were sometimes fights in the Point. I've seen them stripped to the waist to see who was the better man. Oh, yeah. They used to have a tavern at the corner of Congregation and Wellington called The Bucket of Blood. There was a fight every Friday night. We used to bet on them. They used to fight on a dead-end street which ran from Wellington over to Mullins Street. Somebody used to say, "Go over and get the cops. Get the bulls." We used to call them the bulls because they were very powerful men and they worked alone on foot patrol.

My Uncle Mike worked for the Lachine Canal. There was compulsory retirement in those days and, about six months before his sixty-fifth birthday he got a letter saying that he would be retiring. He was still very active and didn't look his age so he went to see Tom Healy, the alderman. Tom Healy had a garage and an office at the corner of Centre and Wellington. Uncle Mike made an appointment and Healy said, "Come in, Mike. Come in." My uncle said, "Tom, I'm going to make it fast. They want to put me out. I'll be sixty-five in six months. Is there anything you can do?" "Well," he said, "I'm going to see the minister of transport and I'll talk to him. I'm not promising anything but tell you what, pass the medical and if you can get a letter from Dr. Duffy that you're O.K. there'll be no problem." My uncle's boss said that he would never get permission but the letter came down from Ottawa and he got a three-year extension. Tom Healy was one of the real old-time Irish politicians. If you had a wooden leg and he wanted to get you in the police or fire department, he'd fight to get you in. He was a fighter and a great man. So was Frank Hogan. Nobody said no to Frank Hogan at City Hall or he'd say, "I won't get me "b'ys" to work for you next election." Tom was quieter and would say, "I think now, Mr. Asselin (or Mr. Houde) that we can compromise. I think that we can maybe…, you know. I'll do that for you and maybe I can do this."

When Frank Hanley started he had no car and I know that he took the streetcar to go down to City Hall with people to help them. He started from the bottom. People who couldn't pay their water tax, he'd have a delay put on it. People with their lights cut off, he'd try to get the money from some organization to help them out. If they needed coal, he'd go to one of the dealers and say, "Could you send a ton of coal." If they needed food, same thing. If they needed a job, he'd go and say, "Why are you turning this man down? He needs the work."

He'd go right to the head of the department.

When I finished school I worked for the City of Montreal as a monitor organizing games in the playgrounds and rinks. I had my application in to become a policeman but you had to be twenty-one years of age to join and the Town of Mount Royal took me at twenty. I was lucky to join because I couldn't drive for five years. In those days you had to be twenty-five to be covered by insurance in the Police and Fire Departments. I did traffic for five years. T.M.R. was very strict on discipline. You couldn't chew gum. You couldn't smoke in uniform. You had to stand erect all the time and it was "Madam" and "Sir." Your sideburns had to be a certain length. There was a "fall in" and a "fall out." The officers were addressed as Sir and you had to wear the uniform home.

When I got in, I liked it. The salary was going up and conditions were changing for the better. When I joined you had to work six days a week; not a four-day week like today. A lot of guys wanted to quit but they were told, "Hang in there. It's getting better." The worst thing about police work today is the shift work.

When you're a police officer, you see and hear everything. You're dispatched to all kinds of problems and you need good self control. When I go up to my locker I take off the uniform and leave everything there. There is a high percentage of police officers who are divorced. A lot of police officers, when they have problems, walk around the block and say, "Hey Paul, let's go have a beer." They sit down there and they don't realize that they're consuming a lot. I'm a non-drinker but a lot of them do it. That's the reason there are a lot of suicides too.

Friday was a popular bank holdup day because the banks always kept a lot of cash on hand. They usually happened before 11 a.m. and so we would check out suspicious cars that were parked in front of banks in the morning. Once the sergeant told me to check out a car at the Rockland Shopping Center. I did and went into the Bank of Montreal where I saw this beautiful, petite woman. She asked me in a very polite way if there was anything wrong. I said, "No, no. It's just a routine check." She said that she was just getting some information and I left. I found out later that she was the notorious Machine Gun Molly. She was probably casing the bank. When I found this out, my hair started to curl because I could have been wiped out in a flash had it been a real holdup. The luck of the Irish was with me that day.

One day I was patrolling solo (a one-man car) and I saw this beautiful lady crossing through the gate in the fence in T.M.R. to get to L'Acadie. Being young, the devil got in me I said, "Oh, nice shape, kid." I wasn't thinking. She was Greek and had to ask someone what those words meant. This was in 1967—Theo and

I got married in 1974! It took me a long time to get married. I lived with my mom and my nephew (my mother reared him from the age of two). My mother wasn't too well and I was helping to support her. What was I going to do? So we waited. I wasn't wishing for her to die and I explained this to Theo. She said, "This is going to go on and on. Your mother could live to be over 100." So I told Ma, "Look, I'm getting engaged," and she said, "Already?" I said, "Ma, I'm forty-three." So that was it. Father Patrick Ryan married us down in St. Gabriel's. We had a nice wedding and every Saturday we'd go down to visit my mother.

Cy Fisher, married at last to Theo. St. Gabriel's Church,
July 20, 1974. His mother is at right.
Courtesy of Cyril Fisher.

Denis Delaney

Denis Delaney has had a chequered career but he has courageously managed to put his life together and lives each day to the full. He was born in Griffintown in 1933 of Irish parents. His father was from Fair Hill, Cork and his mother came from Skibereen. Before his retirement, Denis was the "hands off" manager of the patient-run radio station at the Douglas Hospital. An important part of Denis's life today is the counselling he does with alcoholics.

I was born in a little house on the corner of William Street and Little Eleanor in Griffintown. There's an Eleanor Street where the sisters had the school. That part goes from Ottawa to William and then there's a tiny, little dog leg and then from William Street it runs up to Notre Dame. It's a very narrow street— it wasn't marked Little Eleanor but everyone called it that.

My father could neither read nor write. My mother taught my father with her hand on top of his, how to sign his name. It looked like a three-year-old's signature, wavy and shaky and everything else. That was all he could do. My father was a gentle, intelligent man. He used to carry an eyeglasses case in his pocket and whenever he was with his cronies and somebody would hand him a newspaper and say: "Dinny, did you see this in the paper?" He'd take it, ruffle it and make a big show of it and ask, "Where?" They'd point it out and he'd say, "Just a minute now. I'll get my glasses. Oh, I left them at home again." He didn't want people to know that he couldn't read or write, you see, so he used that for a pretext. He worked as a pick and shovel man for the City of Montreal. It was a political thing in those days. Frank Hanley or O'Connell or one of the local politicians would get you the job. Most of the people worked for the Corporation and they had horses and wagons in those days. My father was an alcoholic like me and my very earliest memories during the Depression were of food. Because he was an alcoholic and spent what little money he got we often went hungry because he didn't bring any money home and there was none of this social stuff like they have today. You had it or you didn't have it. So when he *did* bring the pay home my mother would go out and buy a 75-80 pound bag of potatoes and a lot of dried beans and stuff like that to tide us over until more money came in. Food was important to us. Very, very important.

Women were a lot more subdued in those days although they really ran the show. I think it was like that in Ireland and Griffintown was a microcosm of Ireland. Although the men were out front and were running everything, it was really the women. My mother would wait until my father got sober and he had a big head. Then she would lace into him verbally and he'd say, "O.K. Mary. Never again Mary. I swear. I promise." (laughs)

There were six children in our family. My oldest brother Bill, my sister Mary, the oldest girl, followed by Helen, followed by Julia, followed by Delia and I'm between Helen and Julia. I didn't know we were poor until I was about twelve years old. I did not know what poverty was until outside influences acted on me. I mean, in winter we wore old socks with holes in them as gloves. When our hands were chapped we would go in the lane and pee on them. It worked— burned like hell but it worked. We all did that. There were a lot of similar home remedies. We always wore large boots and then wore them until they pinched our toes. You passed things on in your own family. Today, we put out a lot of garbage. In those days, almost nothing went out. You started out with something and it passed down the line and then, if a neighbour had kids the clothes would fit, they went to the neighbour. If something was really in bad shape it was cut up and used as rags. So very little ended up in the garbage and the same thing for food. Food would end up in the stew pot or the soup pot which went on for weeks on end. I mean you'd have fish in there as a stew which would end up as fish soup and then along would come a ham bone and that was thrown in and it just kept going and going. This pot was usually on the stove all the time.

We were buggers but we wouldn't get into any major trouble. If the baker came by with his wagon with the little doors, we would wait until he went to deliver the bread. There were very few cakes and pies sold in Griffintown in those days. We'd get an apple core and we would hold it in front of the horse's nose and try to entice the old dear to move down the street. Then we'd unlatch the side door and take a pie or a cake. We never stole more than one cake or pie because we knew it was the guy's living. We would steal one and go into the lane and eat it. Same with the peddler or Mr. Stacey, the ice man. He used to come around with his wagon and great blocks of ice on it and we'd go up and chip off a couple of pieces of ice. We'd steal an apple or a potato from the peddler but I can't recall that we would go and take a bag of potatoes. We wouldn't do that. We'd go into Tougas's coal yard on Murray Street at night. We'd go over the fence with rotten meat that we'd find behind Pesner's. We'd throw this rotten meat at the vicious German Shepherd dogs they had. They'd eat you up, those buggers. We'd throw the meat far out and they'd go over and gobble it up. We'd take a coal skuttle, shove it into the pile and pass it up and away we'd go with the coal. But it wasn't for gain. We would bring it home and then we would have to make up a tall story for Mom or she'd bring it back to Tougas's the next day.

Brother Norbert had a great influence on my life. He was a big monster of a man. He walked in to school one day, lined us all up, came to the first one and said: "do, re, mi, fa, so, la, ti, do" and we all had to do it. We were told: "You're in the choir." We weren't asked. He taught me a love of music and made me understand discipline for the first time in my life. He taught me that music is not totally emotional. I think that up until that point that's what it was to me. I loved music all my life and he taught me that there was a definite discipline to it. He and I were at loggerheads always. It was a love-hate relationship. He really was my pseudo father. I loved the man and I hated his guts. (laughs) When he retired, he went to live in Quebec City. I tried to look him up when I went there on a visit but couldn't find him. I hear he died a few years ago.

I remember D'Arcy Boyle, Frankie Doyle, Allan Young, myself and a few others used to sing the Masses nearly every day and we would get points which, at the end of the year, we could turn into something. I wanted a watch. I don't know why but I wanted a watch. We got our gift at Christmas after the Midnight Mass so at about 1-1:30 in the morning we'd go back to St. Ann's School and they'd dole out these presents that we had earned during the year. Brother Norbert called my name and it wasn't a little box. It was a big package. I went up and got it. It was a winter coat. Well, I refused to take it and I stomped out of the classroom. I had worked all year for this watch and I didn't get the watch. Brother Norbert came by the next day but I wouldn't come downstairs. Finally, he got me at school and demanded that I take the coat. I said: "I will not wear that coat. Absolutely not. I earned the watch and I want my watch." Stubborn Irishman! I never wore that coat. I *would not* wear it. My parents tried to get me to wear that coat but I refused. (laughs)

Initially, we didn't have a bath or shower in our house. When we were small, Mom dumped us in the kitchen sink. We could go to Gallery's Bath or O'Connell's Bath to take a shower and swim. You could only go to O'Connell's three days a week and if you went in the evening you had to pay a nickel or a dime. We would go there and try to avoid washing. They had showers along the wall and Mr. Barry would send us back to wash if we weren't clean enough to go into the pool. After swimming you'd come out and put on your old dirty rags again. But the canal was freedom. That's what the canal was. It was Huckleberry Finn and Tom Sawyer. There were no adults around. You knew there was a lot of danger and you tested it constantly. We used to dive down as far as we could go (about twenty-eight feet in that area) and get a handful of silt to prove we had done it. We'd bring it back up to show the other idiots up there who were going down next. It was very cold and very black. You couldn't see a thing and it was very scary. You weren't going to die but you really could have. Sometimes we'd fake going to the bottom. We'd dive in and go down maybe ten feet and try to get something out from between the big boulders on the side instead of going all the way down. If we had nothing to do, we'd go to the Griffintown Boys' Club. It was just a nice place to go. If school was out and you couldn't get into mischief, well, you went over there to play games and meet friends.

There were several accidents over the years. The Oka Sand company (Consolidated Oka Sand & Gravel Co. Ltd.) had hundreds of tons of sand on their property. As the sand was dropped in, the piles became shaped like peaks. We would climb up these huge piles of sand and fly down. One day a kid was there and he somehow got stuck. The sand completely covered him and he was gone. He died. Another kid drowned in the canal. He dived down between one of the huge barges and the canal wall. The barge moved against the wall and he couldn't come back up.

We used to go to movies when we were about twelve or fourteen years old. You had to be sixteen to get in so we used to put shoe polish cans in our shoes to make us taller. We were kicked out quite often. You could go to the Fairyland Theatre and see three full-length pictures for a quarter. The very first movie I saw there was Desert Fury with Lizabeth Scott and I remember being fascinated by the colour. Old Mickey (he was not quite retarded but he was a bit slow) used to go around selling popcorn. Once a week they would give you dishes and you could literally collect a set; cups, saucers and so on. They also had concert night where they would showcase local talent. I sang there many times. The first prize was two dollars, the second prize was a dollar and the third prize was fifty cents. Usually the guy who owned the theatre would get somebody he knew up who would just squawk things out and win first prize.(laughs)

Nobody that I knew owned a hockey stick. We used broom handles and the puck was usually a lump of coal or a chunk of ice and, if you didn't like playing on one side because the wind was blowing in your face, you changed sides. Sometimes you'd have eight people on one side and one or two guys on the other. Didn't matter. Nobody kept score and we didn't care. When we heard the word "Supper!" everybody dropped everything and headed in to get food.

I remember the plane crash in Griffintown in 1944. I had bummed school and had just come down from the bedroom at a quarter to eleven because I had slept in. I coughed a lot earlier so as not to go to school. We always had a pot of tea going on the stove and I picked it up to go to the kitchen table. I was halfway across with the pot in my hand and the back window blew in. The next thing I remember is I'm standing on the corner of Colborne and Ottawa and right next to me is the principal of the school and the flames are going up and you could hear the screaming and yelling. It was a Polish crew and the plane had crashed into the tenement right across from the Griffintown Boys' and Girls' Club. Fifty-calibre shells were going off all over the bloody place. We could hear the screams of the people. They took the wreck of the plane and moved it across the street and erected a fence around it. We used to sneak over at night and go in and steal parts of the plane. I remember one of my friends got the altimeter. A lot of people went behind the barrier to search even though they had army guards—kids can get in anywhere.

The very first drink I remember taking was at my oldest sister's engagement party where my father went nuts and I remember leaving the house. My father hated the English and my sister wanted to marry a British man. He actually had been a Christian Brother who had taught at St. Ann's School. My sister met him three years after he left the order. My father broke that up and my sister never married. My mother had hired Armand Savoie, the boxer, to play for the party; he was fantastic on the piano accordion. My father came out of the bedroom in his longjohns, screaming and yelling and so on and I remember that I was so deeply embarrassed that I snuck out of the house with another guy. There were all kinds of cases of beer out in the back to keep them cool. We stole a case of beer and went across the street and I remember I drank bottle after bottle after bottle until I got violently ill. That's my first conscious remembrance of using alcohol to blot things out.

I've had, and this is no exaggeration, about 200 jobs in my life. My alcoholism took me down many strange roads. I worked at McGill for a year. I dug graves. I picked apples. I worked for CPR as a yardman. I worked for Monsanto … I'd get a job on a Tuesday or Wednesday, work all week, get my pay, go out and the following Monday I wouldn't even remember where I worked, the name of the company or anything else. Where I really learned my "trade" was in the Canadian Navy. What a place to learn how to be an alcoholic.(laughs) I was in for three years and I asked to get out. I would have been booted out anyway.

I was heading toward death. I knew it. I was actually welcoming death because I was destroying myself and everybody around me. I was down to about 100 pounds, sleeping behind hospital grills or on the canal bank with newspaper stuffed around my body. I was thirty-four when I came out of it. I went to bed on January 3, 1968 and when I woke up on January 4, I knew it was over. I don't know why this happened and I don't care. All I know is that it turned me right around. I was very vulnerable the first year. The normal pattern is that I should have fallen back. I knew I had to get a new philosophy of life and a new morality. I had no one to help me. That's when I started writing. The first thing I wrote was a poem about the assassination of Martin Luther King. I thought it was a garbagey, rambling piece but a friend of mine sent it in to the *Lachine Messenger* and they published it. I went out and got fifty copies. Ego. Ego. Ego. (laughs) Until then I had been like a person stumbling around in a pitch black room for sixteen years and, all of a sudden, his elbow hits the light switch and everything is there.

I started getting involved in things. I was one of the people who started Tel-Aide. I've been involved in projects at Shawbridge and at the Douglas Hospital. Today, I work out of my wallet. I keep no records, no phone numbers. I go when I'm asked to go, do my work and then leave. I utilize AA and speak at their meetings. I speak at high school graduations if they want me to. I will speak anywhere. That's why I'm here. Everything else is secondary. Helping people keeps me sober. The AA philosophy is to live one day at a time and I live life on a second to second basis. I thoroughly enjoy my life.

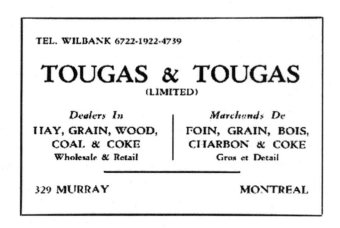

"We'd go into Tougas's coal yard on Murray Street at night…and we'd go away with coal. We would bring it home and then we would have to make up a tall story for Mom."
From Golden Jubilee Souvenir Booklet for the Redemptorist Fathers at St. Ann's, 1934. Courtesy of the Burns family.

Don Pidgeon

Don Pidgeon was born in 1937 and grew up in Griffintown, living there from the 1940s to the mid 1960s. He has been involved in his Irish heritage from kindergarten where he sang and danced with the children at the St. Patrick's Day celebrations at St. Ann's Hall to the present, where he is the historian for the United Irish Societies of Montreal. He was one of the first to challenge the Parks Canada development concept that minimized the Irish impact on Grosse Isle. When the Black Stone Monument lot on Bridge Street was in danger of possible expropriation and deterioration, he negotiated a new fence with the CNR.

My grandfather, William Pidgeon, settled in Williamstown, Ontario and was from Dublin. He met and married a French-Canadian girl, Lina Turcot. My father was their only child and he was sent to Montreal when he was very young after my grandfather died. He was brought up as a French Canadian by a married aunt on his mother's side who had no children of her own. My grandmother was not in a position to take care of a child alone. My father believed he was French Canadian until the time came for him to get a birth certificate and he found out his name was William James Pidgeon. His aunt had always spelled his name as Pigeon. When we were young we spoke English at home since my mother could not speak French, but we spoke French with our father and our cousins. Being bilingual helped me later on in my stage career in Griffintown. They always had me playing the part of a Frenchman.

My father married Marjorie Black from Nova Scotia. She was of Scottish and Irish descent. I'm the youngest. I have two sisters, Thelma and Rita and a brother Bill (William) who was named after my father. Primarily, I identify myself as a Canadian with an Irish heritage. Growing up in Griffintown helped my Irish identification. We moved there in 1940 when I was three years old. Although the neighbourhood was pretty well beginning its decline when I was growing up, there still was a strong community atmosphere with St. Ann's Church, the St. Ann's Young Men's Society, the Holy Name Society and the choir. We also had the Griffintown Boys' and Girls' Club. This club was run by Cliff Sowery and Miss McCunn. They were very involved in the community and did a tremendous job. There was always great respect between these two people and the Catholic community at large. To this day, if I meet Cliff Sowery, he always says that I am one of his boys because I belonged to the Club.

Corpus Christi was celebrated every year with the Blessed Sacrament being carried through certain streets of Griffintown. There was always a big cleanup before Procession Sunday. The buildings were whitewashed or painted, flags

Don Pidgeon, proudly standing beside the renovated Black Stone Monument
on Bridge Street near the entrance to the Victoria Bridge. It marks
the final resting place of thousands of immigrant Irish who died of
typhus after fleeing Ireland's potato famine.
Courtesy of Don Pidgeon.

were hung from windows and banners were stretched across the streets. There would be different flags, the Papal flag, Montreal's flag and Canada's flag which, in those days, was the red ensign. It was a fantastic feeling. There were prayers and the singing of different hymns. The procession would be led off by different societies like the Sodality, the Holy Name Society and would include choirboys and altar boys among others. Then there would be the priests. The sidewalks were filled with people who would fall to their knees as the monstrance would go by. Even the toughest guys would be on their knees and it was quite a religious happening. The procession would end up at the fire station which had been cleaned and painted. The firemen were all waiting there in full dress. It was a wonderful experience.

The house we lived in on Murray Street was owned by a Jewish man but the Irish still owned quite a few of the houses at that time. There were some French owners as well. We lived above a Chinese laundry; the Chinese man who ran the laundry was there when we moved in and he died while we were still in Griffintown. He was a nice man and I learned a few words of Chinese from him. Most of my friends were Irish-Canadian boys. I recall as a youngster that if my friend's mother was out, I'd bring him home to eat and stay with us and he would do the same if my mother was out. The parents were involved with controlling all the children and the older children had a responsibility towards the younger ones to keep them out of trouble. I remember my mother giving food and assistance to people who needed help. To this day, if I meet someone from Griffintown, there's a bond that exists. There's a genuine friendliness and that's something that's always been with us—to co-operate and help each other.

When we were teenagers we would go to St. Eustache Beach with a group of fellows and girls on Saturdays or Sundays. We'd take the train and spend the day. If we stayed with a family we would go for the weekend. We also had a lot of parties because we belonged to different groups. Parties were the "in" thing for young people. At home we had two pianos because both my sisters played. My brother played the guitar and harmonica. My father could play practically any instrument so we did a lot of entertaining at home.

There are so many legends in Griffintown. One of them is the headless woman. The story goes that Mary Gallagher was a "lady of the evening" and she was living with another woman who was approximately ten years her junior. They had picked up this man at one of the hotels in the St. James Street area and brought him to their home where much alcohol was consumed. During the course of the evening, the younger woman became jealous of the older one, for some reason or another, and took an axe and cut Mary's head off. The head was supposed to have been put into a bucket and this was the start of the legend that every seven years, Mary Gallagher would come back looking for her head. This story happened in the late 1800s. The house where Mary Gallagher was murdered was near the corner of William and Murray, just up the street from where we lived. During the summer months I recall we would not go up Murray Street. We would go blocks around to avoid that area. There was a genuine fear. There was another very old house on Murray Street where an elderly lady lived with her son. We all thought she was a witch and were afraid to pass by her house.

One of the houses we lived in was haunted. Every Friday evening my aunts would come over to visit my mother and they would have tea downstairs and we kids would play. The bathroom was upstairs. One night my sister Rita and my cousin Pauline went up to go to the bathroom. Now the door to the bathroom had a part at the bottom that you could see through and they swear to this day that there was a man in the bathroom. They could see the pant legs and the feet of a man. They ran downstairs and my mother and aunts came up carrying pokers and knives but there was no one there. In that same house, when I was a baby, my crib was placed just at the top of the stairs and I had a blanket that went missing. A while later, my sister Thelma saw the blanket hanging on the side of the crib. She ran to grab the blanket and, as she did so, it went right down and into the floor and was never found. We at times had very unnerving experiences in that house.

There were some people in Griffintown who had a different lifestyle, of course. On Friday night, some of the men would get drunk and roll home. Certain women could beat the hell out of these men. I remember one woman, who went down to beat her drunken husband with a baseball bat and when her brother jumped in to try to stop her, she beat him too. Did men beat their wives in Griffintown? I would presume it went on as it does in all societies but it was a different way of living then. The families all lived in the community and I think a lot of men would hold back on beating their wives because her brothers could come over and beat him too. So I think that put a certain restraint on things. Remember, too, the strength of the priests who used to walk around the community. I remember Father Kearney (who was the heart and soul of Griffintown) walking around with his cane. These priests walked around and spoke to people. They went into the homes and they had tea with many families. Their involvement in the lives of the people probably stopped a lot of aggressive behaviour.

There was a place called Frank's Grocery Store on the southwest corner of Ottawa and Murray. Frank was Lebanese, the first man from Lebanon that I ever met in my life. He was a very quiet, gentle man. Anyway, there was this large, Irish woman who would walk in to buy beer. She could handle a wooden case filled with twelve quarts of beer. I remember being in the store one day when she walked in and banged this case of empties on the counter. The thunder of it shook everything in the place and we were all scared. In her Irish brogue she yelled out to Frank, "Frank, would ye be givin' me twelve Black Arse beer." For the longest period of time I thought it was Black Arse beer, not Black Horse beer.

The 24th of May (the Queen's birthday) was not a good time for policemen and firemen. The kids would start fires on one corner and while the Police and Fire Departments were busy with the first fire, they would start another one three blocks away. I remember the boys saving up old tires, chesterfields and chairs that had been thrown out during the year. They'd hold on to these things until the 24th of May. It was difficult being a policeman in Griffintown because many of the people had a distaste for them. The firemen fared better, perhaps, because the Fire Department was where a lot of the Irish boys wanted to be.

Expo 67 was about the end of things. They tore down a lot of buildings in Griffintown when they built the Bonaventure overpass and Goose Village as such was finished when they put up the stadium. Right up until the end, St. Ann's Church kept attracting people to the Mother of Perpetual Help devotions.

I'd like to finish by singing you a song we used to sing in Griffintown:

> Griffintown, Griffintown,
> That's where I long to be
> Where my friends are good to me
> Hogan's Bath on Wellington Street
> Where the Point bums wash their feet
> Haymarket Square, I don't care anywhere
> For it's Griffintown for me. (laughs)

Brother Jeffries at the head of a large contingent of altar boys from
St. Ann's Church in the Corpus Christi Procession, June 19, 1938.
All the societies and groups in the parish, such as the Holy Name
Society, and the Sodality would participate in the show of faith
which would wend its way through certain streets of
the neighbourhood.
Photo by Kay Peachey.

This photograph, taken in 1939 shows a few of the well-known priests who were active in Montreal parishes for many years. Father Healy was born on Laprairie Street in Point St. Charles in what was known as the "Kerry Patch."
(left to right) Fr. John O'Rourke, Fr. James O'Toole, Fr. John Ryan, Fr. Gerald Britt, Fr. Michael Healy
Courtesty of Reverend Michael Healy.